A HEALER'S JOURNEY
INTO LIGHT

A HEALER'S JOURNEY INTO LIGHT

Lorna Todd

BANTAM BOOKS

TORONTO • NEW YORK • LONDON • SYDNEY • AUCKLAND

A HEALER'S JOURNEY INTO LIGHT
A BANTAM BOOK: 0 553 40851 8

Originally published in Great Britain by Bantam Press,
a division of Transworld Publishers Ltd

PRINTING HISTORY
Bantam Press edition published 1995
Bantam edition published 1996

Set in 10/11pt Linotron Sabon by Falcon Oast Graphic Art

Bantam Books are published by Transworld Publishers Ltd,
61–63 Uxbridge Road, Ealing, London W5 5SA,
in Australia by Transworld Publishers (Australia) Pty Ltd,
15–25 Helles Avenue, Moorebank, NSW 2170,
and in New Zealand by Transworld Publishers (NZ) Ltd,
3 William Pickering Drive, Albany, Auckland.

Reproduced, printed and bound in Great Britain by
Cox & Wyman Ltd, Reading, Berks.

This book is dedicated to my beloved mother, Phoebe Curry, who recently passed over into the light. The love and beauty which shone from her soul was an inspiration to all who met her.

ACKNOWLEDGEMENTS

My first and very special thanks go to my husband Peter, without whose help and love this book would never have been written.

I am indebted to Sheila and Alfred Miller, Joan Fugeman and all my many friends, whose names would fill several pages. These companions surrounded my work with light and positive thoughts, never losing their faith in my ability to act as a channel for this book.

My gratitude goes out to Grace and Ivan Cooke, Joan, John, Ylana, Jenny, Geoffrey, Colum, Jeremy, Anna, Avis and Jean Le Fevre, whose devotion to the work of White Eagle Lodge has enabled thousands of people to open up their hearts as centres for love and light on the surface of this beautiful planet we call Earth.

My appreciation is also felt for Patricia Mitchell and Edmund Harold, whose special insight pointed me in the right direction when my feet were faltering. This also extends to all my friends in the 'Spheres of Light', whose guidance managed to reach me when my faith and inspiration wavered.

Lastly, I would like to express my grateful thanks to Mark Barty-King, Jennie Bull, Brenda Kimber and all their colleagues at Bantam Press who have treated me with such kindness and understanding. It is their unshakeable confidence and hard work that has made this publication a reality.

CONTENTS

AUTHOR'S NOTE

I feel that it is important to point out that the thoughts and views expressed in this book do not necessarily represent the beliefs of the White Eagle Lodge, the Sussex Healers or the National Federation of Spiritual Healers.

Lorna Todd

PREFACE

by PATRICIA MITCHELL
(a well-known Sussex Astrologer)

Dear Reader,

In these days of disbelief in any true reason for happiness or contentment, it is my pleasure to write a short preface to introduce you to Lorna.

We have been friends for over twenty years, each travelling a different way to gain a small glimpse of the eternal.

My road has been through the study of Astrology, which, contrary to popular belief, does not mean that your complete life is mapped out for you. We all have choices and free will. For instance, Lorna was born in the sunny month of August (Leo), which is a good description of her. However, she could have chosen to be bossy and dogmatic.

Another important part of any Astrological reading is in the moon sign. Lorna's moon falls in the psychic sign of Scorpio, where her considerable

13

talent for healing has its roots. Just as easily she would be able to use this power negatively. In all the years I have known Lorna, this has never happened.

When you have incidents which are difficult to explain, it is easy to feel fear of rejection and ridicule. However, more and more people are crying out for knowledge and it is that impetus which has encouraged Lorna to put her particular experiences down on paper, for you to share.

I am sure that Lorna's story will inspire you to have confidence in your future, and renewed hope for a better world.

INTRODUCTION

Although I have always been able to express myself fairly well by the spoken word, the idea of a written text had never occurred to me. Not, that is, until I began to encounter strong images and symbols during meditation. I would see books with open blank pages, waiting for me to fill them with writing from an old-fashioned pen and ink pot. I would be shown a picture of myself as a young schoolgirl sitting at a small, badly scratched desk, chewing the end of my pencil. Slowly it filtered through to me that the White Brotherhood wanted me to write a book. For a long while I ignored these impressions. It wasn't something that I wished to undertake as I had too many other commitments all bidding for my time. The pictures, however, got stronger and more insistent, even impinging on my dreams. Eventually I gave way, remembering the words, 'Not my will, but thine.'

It became apparent that the Brotherhood wanted me to write a story of my life on the healing path, telling of my many experiences in this world and the next, taking into account other lives spent on other continents. It was impressed upon me that it must be written with great love from the heart. The words that came to me were:

> The Masters, who watch over mankind at the present time, are concerned that Searchers on the path are opening up their brow and head centres before the heart centre is fully awakened. This can cause damage and hinder their progression on the journey of spiritual evolution.

Whilst I was pondering the implications of my meditations, I remembered the words of a wise woman who gave me direction nearly thirty years ago. She had a vision, in which she saw me surrounded by piles and piles of papers. She also said that I was working on a strange machine which looked like a typewriter. I am now sure that what she was describing was my word processor, thirty years into the future.

We are on the brink of a New Age called Aquarius. During this period of approximately 2,000 years, our level of consciousness will be raised. We will be living on a higher level of vibration. This will bring to mankind many advantages. We will begin to exist in a positive and loving manner. Sharing and unity with all creation on Mother Earth will be our normal expression. The Golden Age for humanity will have arrived.

I am aware of the fact that I have been guided during the preparation of this book and I hope you will find it absorbing and interesting. You may not share some of my views and beliefs. That doesn't matter. My truth may not be your truth — there are many roads back to God. I only ask that you read my words with an open mind and file away into your subconscious anything that you cannot accept. This may ring true for you at a later date.

Agreement or disagreement is not important. If, by the time you have read all these pages, I have helped you to expand your heart centre and to feel love and unity towards your fellow creatures, then I will have performed my task for the Lords of Light.

I, therefore, invite you to accompany me on my Journey into Light.

A HEALER'S JOURNEY
INTO LIGHT

FOOTSTEPS ON THE PATH

FOOTSTEP 1

A Young Spark

'Mum,' I implored, 'can Mary come to tea?' My poor mother sighed. 'Yes dear,' she replied and laid another place at the table for my invisible friend who only I could see. As a single child I had made quite sure, when venturing once more into incarnation, that I would never be lonely. I had brought back with me, from the land of spirit, children who would come and be my companions whenever I needed them. Mary was a small pretty little girl with long blond ringlets. 'Why is it that I can see her so clearly and no-one else can?' I asked myself.

The ancient wisdom teaches us that when God made man, he breathed us forth as little sparks of himself to start our journey through the planes of consciousness, arriving eventually on our planet Earth in human form. Man has travelled far since those distant days and through many, many lifetimes has reached the most dense point in his earthly experiences. In other words he can sink no further into physical matter and must start his pilgrimage on the path back to the Godhead.

The spiritual law 'As above, So below' works out through man's life from birth to death. What he experiences in earthly form is mirrored on all other levels of existence. Man arrives as a babe with much to learn, growing to manhood and reaching old age having been through many situations, good and bad, all of which are reflected in his soul's growth. It is said that we are 'Gods in the Making' and that it is man's destiny to become a model of his Maker, a creation of pure love which is the light of Christ. The message is so simple – just love – but, oh, so difficult. When we have grasped this lesson, we will no longer have the need to journey on the wheel of rebirth.

I am telling my story through this book, in an endeavour to help all people who are treading the road with me. I liken the path to Jacob's ladder. There are many in front of me, much more advanced, who stretch down to give me a hand. I in turn reach over to help those who are climbing behind me. I hope you will enjoy my story and begin to realize what a wonderful inheritance awaits the whole of humanity. At the end of every chapter I have included a meditation, each of which is designed to gently open up the heart centre.

Looking back to my childhood I can't remember a time when I didn't believe in life after death, or reincarnation. I was very fortunate to have been born into a family where, although my mother was Church of England, my aunt, uncle and grandmother were all spiritualists. I was never told that I had a too-vivid imagination, or that I was making things up. I was born on 3 August 1938 in a small village called Kingston Buci, on the south coast of England. Much of my childhood was spent, therefore, during the war. My father marched off to the battlefields of France when I was one year old and I didn't see him again until a strange man carrying a kitbag arrived home when I was about eight.

I was brought up by my mother and grandmother, spending some of the war years in Sussex, but most of the time on my Uncle Tom's farm at Ashill in Norfolk. In this idyllic setting I milked cows, collected eggs and roamed free in the meadows and pastures. The words battery hen and factory farming were unheard of. Time ambled slowly along, the seasons rotating from ploughing time to harvest time. A small single-decker bus ran once a week, on a Wednesday, to the city of Norwich. My Aunt Ethel, my mother and I would saunter down the road to the bus stop, only to see the back of it vanishing round the corner. 'Never mind,' my aunt would say, 'we'll catch it next week.' Apart from a few aircraft, life was peaceful and time went serenely on its way.

Back home, however, the sky was not quite so placid. Sussex was one of the arenas for the Battle of Britain. Like most children I knew little fear and enjoyed the excitement of living in air-raid shelters. What fun lessons were when conducted from a dusty brickbuilt shelter with a tin roof. We even had one at home, which resided in my mother's front room, covered in curtains and cushions. If a bomb had dropped on us we would have roasted alive. Destiny, however, had other work for me to do and the bombers passed safely overhead.

I did not come into this world as an only child.

My mother had given birth prematurely to twins – myself and Marilyn Joy, my sister. We were born in a small cottage next to a church, on a leyline. It was later discovered that my mother's bed had been placed directly over a disused well. The ancient energies flowing through me at birth were to link me all my life to spiritual and angelic forces, enabling me to see and work with these beings of light and love.

I survived the very difficult ordeal of entry into this world, but my twin sister gave up the struggle and returned to spirit after only two days. A medium has since told me that Marilyn had previewed her forthcoming life whilst in the womb and decided that she couldn't face the lessons she would have had to learn – she hadn't been strong enough. I, on the other hand, had looked at my oncoming life and chosen to stay and work my karma through. For many years I felt Marilyn's presence until suddenly her nearness left me. I realized that she had again incarnated, with enough will this time to complete her destiny. I have been told where she is, so I can keep my eye on her without intruding or interfering with her free will.

Owing to my arduous and painful birth, my mother could have no more children and for a number of years I was a very sickly child. At birth my grandmother and my Aunt Sheila kept me alive by laying me in cotton wool and feeding me with a fountain pen filler. There were no incubators in 1938. My entry into this realm of consciousness, although formidable, had been blessed with love. I was often very ill and up to the age of seven pneumonia, scarlet fever, measles and chickenpox took their toll. I looked death in the face several times but pulled through with the help of a splendid man called Dr Dobbin and a devoted family.

Nowadays many people have told of their encounters with the tunnel of light through 'near death' experiences. This was a familiar happening to me, which didn't occur at 'near death', but on most nights, just as I was falling asleep. I can still see the revolving wheel of light; a blaze of intermingling colours combining all the different shades of the rainbow. As I progressed through the tunnel, these colours changed to a pure white light – the light and love of Christ. My journey took me to a place of green fields, birds, animals and sunlight. There I played with other children from spirit until it was time to awaken and I found myself once more in my own bed and well-known surroundings. I was aware of these friends during my waking hours and thought everyone could see them. It was a great shock to me when I realized that they remained unseen to other people.

When I was about two years old, my mother decided to move and we went to live in the next village, called Southwick. The house my mother chose was part of a terrace and, after I started school, the home next to us became vacant. Before long a couple with a little girl, a few years older than myself, moved in. Her name was Cleo and we quickly became firm friends. She had a clever mind which, unfortunately, occupied a very frail body. She suffered with dreadful asthma attacks that left her frequently fighting for breath. As the years passed the asthma assaults became more numerous and her heart became weaker. At twelve years of age her body gave up the battle for life and she died. My mother met me from school and told me the sad news.

That night, as I was about to fall asleep, I became aware of the figure of Cleo standing beside my bed. It came as no surprise when she joined me on my journey, through the tunnel, into the spheres of light. She was so happy with no more pain and suffering. 'Look,' she said, 'I can breathe at last.' Her whole spiritual body glowed with beauty. If only her parents could have seen her joy, their grieving would have been so much less.

I wouldn't like it to be thought that I spent all my childhood with my head in the heavens. Most of the time I was a tomboy with my feet firmly on the ground; no tree was too tall for me to climb, no adventure too dangerous for me to attempt. I much preferred cars and roller skates to dolls and cradles. After the war there was very little danger to our physical bodies so my human friends and I roamed fields, downlands and beaches engaged in games of Tarzan, Dick Barton special agent and cowboys and indians.

There was one incident, however, during our pursuits, when my guardians in spirit came to my rescue. I was one of about a dozen children enjoying ourselves on the Sussex downs. We were playing 'tag' which is a variation of 'hide and seek'. I was crouched behind a gorse bush when I suddenly heard a voice in my ear telling me to turn round. On doing so, I discovered that I was not alone. Kneeling behind me was a naked man who was just about to grab me. I let out a piercing scream, took to my heels and ran as fast as I could down the hill. The other children on hearing my shrill warning came charging down behind me. We had all been badly frightened and without the warning in my ear I dread to think what might have happened. My invisible helpers had worked very hard on that day to keep me secure.

There were several occurrences in my childhood, when I 'saw' not just with my inner eye but with my physical eyes as well. The terraced cottage where we lived had been built about thirty years before my mother moved in. This house has always had an atmosphere of peace and protection that is due, I am sure, to the presence of my friend 'the lady with the brush and dustpan'. I first met her when I was about six years old. I came out of the upstairs bathroom and saw this 'lady' sweeping the stairs and landing. At first I thought it was my mother, but I then heard my mum downstairs in the kitchen, washing up, and I realized that this was another 'friend'. She watched over me when I was young and also in later years when, in great trouble, I came home to stay for a short while.

I was constantly aware of my 'lady' and I am not surprised that my parents have never wanted to live anywhere else in Southwick. It is only right that my mother should have such a 'protector', as she herself is a very lovely and advanced soul. To my knowledge she has never harmed anyone in thought, word or deed.

Another memory of childhood was the fact that I could levitate and I used this method many times to get down the stairs quickly. This was something, however, that I kept to myself without sharing it with the adults. It was my secret and at the time seemed quite natural. What bliss to just float lightly above the ground. With the onset of puberty this ability left me; the world is not yet ready for adults who can 'fly'.

During the war a large number of Canadian servicemen were billeted in our area. Most of them were extremely young and very homesick. The local people tried to remedy the situation by inviting them into their homes. The result of this was that several Canadians came to tea and stayed the night in our spare room. I spent many a happy early morning jumping into their bed demanding a story. How patient they were with me, when I am sure all they wanted to do was sleep. There was no risk of danger for children from those soldiers, just gifts of chocolates, gum and lots of play and fun. I remember Tom, Ace and others who left our house and shores to meet their deaths on the battlegrounds of Italy.

After the war, I was allowed to sit in 'circle' with my grandmother, Aunt Sheila and the English soldier she had married, Uncle Alf. The method used for communication was a glass that moved round a circle of letters, spelling out words and messages from the world of spirit. I would stress that this method of talking to 'the other side' can be dangerous if used for selfish reasons, as a bit of a laugh, or out of curiosity. When I sat as a child, it was done with prayer and great love. A number of those Canadian soldiers who had died on the battlefields came to talk to us. They spoke to us of personal things that only we could have known, so it is not surprising that I grew up with no doubts about survival of the spirit and life eternal.

When I was ten years old, I was fortunate in obtaining a scholarship to Worthing High School for Girls. At that institution I learned discipline and a love for books, History, English and debating, all of which were to be of enormous help to me in my later life. It was at the end of my last year at school that I encountered, for the first time in this incarnation, negative forces.

A school trip for senior pupils had been arranged to Austria. We were to stay a fortnight in Salzburg, where the Mozart music festival was taking place. The two weeks passed all too quickly and I had a wonderful time enjoying all the sights and sounds of that beautiful city. At the end of the last week a coach trip was organized to Berchtesgaden, with the specific purpose of visiting Hitler's underground bunker. All went well until it was time for me to enter this concrete monolith. The year was 1954, just nine years after the end of the war, so the bunker still retained its awesome vibrations. I walked through the cold and dreary passages feeling sick and faint until I suddenly stopped and could go no further. It was just as if I had come up against a brick wall. My body felt clammy and my legs turned to jelly. I was aware of the smell of rotten vegetables, the stink of which I would, from that day, always associate with evil. Whatever had happened on that spot was reaching out to me, filling me with a terror that I didn't understand. Noticing my ashen face, one of the teachers led me out of the bunker into the clean, fresh air. Many years passed before I could finally comprehend what I had encountered, but it has now been hinted that the bunker was used, by the Nazis, for satanic rites.

My childhood days were soon over and my teenage years came and passed. My interest became centred on boys and dancing rather than on other realms of consciousness, which was a much more healthy outlook for a young girl. It was the era of teddy boys and jiving at Brighton's Regent and Aquarium ballrooms to the sound of Johnny Dankworth. We all screamed and swooned at the crooning of Johnny Ray and Frankie Laine. I took a secretarial course and started work in a busy office. It was there that I was taught a hard lesson that I was never to forget.

One of the senior members of the staff took a strong dislike to me and went out of his way to be offensive and rude. I had been away sick with a bad and painful tooth and on my return he refused to believe that I had been ill at all. I left his office in a terrible rage and proceeded to curse and wish him all manner of terrible afflictions. The very next day he suffered a mild heart attack and collapsed. The hospital couldn't understand why it had happened as he was a very fit man. But I knew and was aghast at what I had done. Fortunately he fully recovered and I had learnt a valuable lesson. I realized how potent my thoughts were and from that day on I have guarded them very carefully.

Not long after I started work, I met and married my husband Peter. He was ex-RAF and very practical. He didn't believe in 'life after death'; 'Dust to dust and ashes to ashes and that's it,' he would say. When I first started to train as a healer, his party piece would be, 'She'll be walking on water next, ha, ha.' Despite this he has never stopped me pursuing my spiritual work and in fact has brought many people to me for help over the years. We have now been married for thirty-four years and he has given me all his support and encouragement during the preparation of this book. Without his help I would never have been able to walk with such large strides on my path of light.

I love him dearly and tell him that if he passes into spirit first, he will think of me saying, 'I told you so – there is no such thing as death.' He is a thoroughly good man who will help anyone. The path he is walking back to God will differ from mine, but the seeds that I have sown for him in this life will bear fruit in his next incarnation. We have met in previous lives and will meet again in future ones, until all the lessons that we have to teach one another have been learnt and the Lords of Karma are satisfied with the results.

THE CANDLE FLAME

The first of our meditations is designed to begin gently to open up your heart centre. Sit in a comfortable straight-backed chair with your spine erect. Lay your hands softly in your lap with the palms upwards. Relax and be at peace. For a little while forget all your troubles and problems; just enjoy the short journey you are about to take into the realms of light. Close your eyes and breathe a little bit deeper.

Use your imagination and see with your inner vision a path in front of you leading into a wood. As you start to walk along this path be aware of the beauty of the trees on either side of you. Magnificent oaks, elms and beech trees are spreading their branches above your head to make an archway over the path. It is a beautiful sunny day and the light from the sun is glinting through the trees. On the ground around the trees you will see spring flowers, clumps of daffodils, violets and primroses. Pause for a moment and listen to the song of the birds. Is that a blackbird or a nightingale that you can hear? For a moment glimpse the small wild animals of this wood: rabbits, squirrels, field mice and hedgehogs. Do you see that a mole has appeared, poking his large paws out from a pile of soil? The animals are not afraid of you, for here they only live with light and love.

Continue your journey until you come to the end of the trees. In front of you, a short distance away, you will see a small hill. Keep walking along your path, climbing slightly until you come to a tiny cave let into the hillside. The interior is not dark, but appears to be lit by all the various shades of the spectrum. Step through the opening and look around the walls where crystals of many shapes and sizes are inlaid. This is where the colours are streaming from, so stand in the centre of the cave and become immersed in the beauty of their radiance.

In front of you is a golden altar, on the top of which burns a small white candle. Kneel before the altar and gaze at the glowing flame. As you look into the light you will become aware that it is expanding and growing. The cavern represents the beauty of your own heart centre and the flame from the candle is the spark of God – the love of God which is in all men. Can you ever be angry again, or jealous of anybody, when you look at the pure wonder of your own temple?

As you watch the blaze from this pure white candle grow larger, it is as if your heart is also opening and widening. Just like the ripples on a pond, the waves from the flame in your own heart centre are spreading outwards, leaving the cavern and reaching out into the world. Send this light to any part of the globe that you know to be in need of healing, or any person you perceive to be in trouble, enfolding and cradling them in this love. Before you leave your temple, pause for a while, and give thanks to our creator for the glorious gift that has flowed from you onto the planet Earth.

The vision of the altar and the cavern slowly begins to fade and as you turn away from the hill you find yourself once more on the path, which leads you back into the wood. Take your time as you walk through the trees, halting for a moment to look at the beauty of nature. Breathe deeply the pure fresh air, inhaling the wondrous scent from the spring flowers.

When you are ready, become aware of your chair, feel the seat beneath you and the floor under your feet. Bring the love and peace back with you into your physical life. Remember that you can return to the cave at any time you wish; it is a part of you and can be made more beautiful each time you visit it.

Before you open your eyes, imagine that a large cross of light within a circle of light is surrounding and enfolding your whole body. This is God's protection as you come back into the reality of your everyday life.

FOOTSTEP 2

Training as a Healer

People often ask me, 'how do I become a healer?' The answer is so simple. Everyone possesses the ability to heal – every mother who kisses her child's grazed knee to make it better is using this faculty. When someone approaches you with a sorry tale to tell and you listen sympathetically, again you are using this spiritual energy.

If you have love for your fellow man or creature all you need to do is open up your heart and let the power of love flow from you to the patient. Love, which is the light of God, is invincible; nothing in this world, or the next, can stand against it. Love will always overcome darkness, and when you walk in its radiance there is nothing to fear, not illness, not death, not poverty. I hope that by the time you have finished this book you will understand and practise this within your personal life and picture your own pathway lit before you.

I didn't commence my training as a channel for

healing until I was about thirty-five. My husband and I had moved back to Southwick to live near my mother and father. My Aunt Sheila, who has always been my confidante and very true friend, knew of my interest in healing. She had seen an advertisement that said a healing clinic was being opened at the Community Centre in Southwick every Monday evening. We decided to go and investigate and, as I was suffering from haemorrhoids, I thought that some help with this condition would also be an added blessing.

This was my first meeting with Ken and Irene Harrison, who were starting the clinic. I would like to pay tribute to these two lovely souls; without their help my journey into light would not have begun. The clinic ran for eight years and during that time many hundreds of people passed through their hands. No-one was turned away, even if it meant working until very late. Every one of those people received aid, in some way or another. Even if a condition could not be cured, the patients went home feeling much happier and more able to cope with their lives. Someone had had time to listen to their sadness and had shown love towards them. It was not surprising that Monday evenings became more and more popular. Seventeen years ago, however, there was still a lot of prejudice with regard to alternative medicine. Our local vicar voiced his opinion that only ordained ministers should practise the laying-on of hands and two elderly ladies wrote to Ken and Irene expressing their concern that healing was indeed the 'work of the devil'. A sense of humour saved the day and, as I have already said, the clinic flourished for a further eight years.

Sheila and I arrived at the Community Centre

on that Monday evening, found the appointed room, entered and sat down. There were already a number of people gathered and soon the room began to fill up. We waited patiently as each person took his turn and as I watched Ken and Irene pass their hands over different bodies, I was aware that the palms of my hands were tingling and feeling very hot. Before long it was my turn and I went and sat down in front of Irene. As she worked on me I felt a gentle heat flow over me and a feeling of deep peace. It was a beautiful experience, which resulted in the complete cure of my very uncomfortable piles. After Irene had finished giving me treatment, Ken walked over to where I was sitting, looked at me and said, 'You should be doing this. Would you like to join us as a probationer and learn to become a healer?' Of course I said, 'Yes, please,' and it was the start of several happy years training and working at the clinic on Monday evenings. I joined the National Federation of Spiritual Healers as a probationer and eventually qualified as a full healer. I later worked with a small but loving band of healers known as The Sussex Healers.

Nobody could have had a better training ground. During those eight years many people passed through my hands, with a wide variety of ailments from impotence to the big 'C' – cancer. We only had one room, so patients would sit in rows waiting for their turn. Some evenings thirty or more people would arrive and it would become a bit noisy. I learnt very early in my training to seal myself off in a pyramid of light. I visualize myself and my patient encased in a triangle of light so that I am only aware of the soul sitting in front of me and can completely cut out any disturbance. I was taught to attune or 'plug in' to the healing power, so that it became automatic and required little thought. All healers have their own method of doing this; I have always formed the figure of the Master Jesus and asked that his healing power flow through my hands to the person in need.

This method of attunement was given to me at the start of my training. I had borrowed a book by Harry Edwards, whom many feel was the greatest healer of this century. In it he explained a simple way of tuning in to give absent healing – the process by which help is sent out, at a distance, through meditation. Harry suggested that you sat down in a comfortable chair and brought into your inner vision a picture of the Master Jesus alleviating the pain of a sick human being.

I did as Harry advised, shut my eyes and immediately found myself in Jerusalem 2000 years ago. I was standing looking at a huge temple, in front of which had gathered a large crowd of people. I managed to push my way through to the first row and beheld a dark-haired man in a white robe holding his hands over the eyes of a blind, poorly dressed beggar. I knew immediately that I was looking at Jesus, as all around him was an aura of light that seemed to grow and grow until it enfolded all the waiting multitude. He turned his head and gazed at me, the love flowing from his eyes holding mine, and I felt my heart centre expand and open. The blind beggar suddenly shouted with delight. For the first time in many years, he could see. Through this wonderful meditation I had my light source to plug into.

At this point I started an absent healing list and set aside half an hour each day to ask for help for the sufferers on my file. I would tune in and hold the sick patient, human or animal, in the light of Christ. I was amazed at the results; it seemed that I was permanently connected. I have a very bad memory and I would sometimes meet someone out shopping who, knowing that I was working as a healer, would ask for a friend or relative to be put on my list. A few weeks later I would see that person again and they would say, 'Thank you so much for helping Aunty Grace, she is feeling a lot stronger.' To my horror, I would realize that I had completely forgotten to include her name. I am sure that once you start working in this way, it is like a radar system; all calls for assistance are picked up and relayed to the appropriate helpers and angels.

Some people react more strongly to absent healing than to bodily contact. My husband is a good example of this. He is a diabetic and a few years ago started to develop bad arthritis in his hands, arms and hips. He wouldn't sit still long enough to gain benefit from physical treatment, so I worked on him from a distance. Within a short while the pain had eased and after about two months the arthritis had completely vanished and has never recurred.

Anybody can practise absent healing and I would urge all readers of this book to try it for themselves. You can use it to help humans, animals, countries, the planet Earth and anything or anyone you know to be in trouble. It is said, 'As you give, so shall you receive,' and I believe this to be true. You will start to feel much happier and healthier. Your step will quicken and you will begin to realize that it is good to be alive. In assisting others you are helping yourself.

There are a large number of lessons to be learnt on the spiritual path, one of which is dispassionate compassion. You have to acquire the ability to withdraw your own emotions or you will become drained. This lesson was brought home to me very early on in my training. My husband came home one day and asked me if I would go and see the wife of a workmate of his, who was suffering from cancer. Naturally I went and for the first time met Lorraine. She was a pretty girl in her early twenties, with two small children. She had been diagnosed as having cancer of the womb and was very swollen with water retention. She was attending the hospital for chemotherapy, which was making her vomit every half an hour. I gave her healing and the pain eased. She told me next day that the sickness had stopped and that she felt much calmer.

Over the following few months I visited her three or four times a week and we became very good friends. I also involved myself with her family and frequently sat with her while her husband went down to the local pub for a drink. I really thought that the healing would cure her and ignored the fact that she was getting weaker and weaker. When she was eventually taken into a hospice I was devastated. I was told that her body was riddled with tumours, and by the time I first arrived to give her help her vital organs had already been badly affected. What the healing had done, however, was to remove most of the pain, bring her peace of mind and make her transition into the world of light so much easier. It was a hard lesson to come to terms with, but an important one. On reflection, however, I realized that part of the joy of being a healer was to bring light and comfort to the dying. What more could you do to aid another soul than to assist them to pass effortlessly through the 'door' onto the other side.

I cannot leave this subject without mentioning the Bristol Clinic, who have worked so hard and valiantly with so many terminally ill people. Usually patients visit the Clinic when the hospitals have sent them home to die. At Bristol they are given healing, a strict vegetarian diet and are taught to visualize their cancer as having left their bodies. They are encouraged to think positively and are surrounded with comfort and hope. I am on the Bristol Clinic's list of healers and over the years have given help to a number of their patients. It is a privilege to watch their change of attitude and to see how decisive they become. The fear of the word 'cancer' has left them and they are open to the recuperative energies which flow through their bodies. Some pass over, but a considerable number are still alive five to ten years after going to the Clinic.

As an example, I will tell the story of John. He had fallen ill and his wife Heather, who was a District Nurse, was shocked when John was diagnosed as having a tumour on the lung. The hospital said that he only had a few months to live and had sent him home with instructions for Heather to make him as comfortable as possible. She immediately took him for the weekend to the Bristol Clinic, where they started his treatment. Combined with regular visits to Bristol, John then came to our clinic in Southwick every Monday evening, where we continued to give him spiritual healing. He found the mainly raw vegetarian diet a problem to start with, but then his whole family joined in, which made it a lot easier.

He first came to our clinic about ten years ago and up to a few weeks ago he was still walking about Southwick. He still had the cancer but for all those years it had been in remission. Unfortunately, whilst writing this chapter I have been told that he has passed over. I am sure John would wish me to include his story as a tribute to the Bristol Clinic. When I saw him a short while ago he said to me, 'If I die tomorrow, I will have had all those extra years.' From two months, which was the hospital's prognosis, to ten years is not a bad recommendation.

When dealing with cancer it is essential that patients keep a positive attitude. Each small cell of our bodies has its own brain, which runs out of control when a cell becomes rampant. Our own main brain must, therefore, be decisive enough to clear cancer from the damaged cells. This is why the beneficial meditations taught at Bristol are so important.

As we have looked at the positive side of cancer I will just mention one of the negative aspects. The power of the mind is so strong that it is possible to will yourself into creating this dis-ease. Worry and think about it enough and the body will react accordingly. I had a very dear friend called Ruby, who was a very spiritual lady. Unfortunately, however, there was something in her make-up which urged her towards self-destruction. When she was in her seventies she developed an obsession with tumours and she was convinced that she had this sickness within her womb. In a short while this fact, combined with other problems, affected her mental stability and she was admitted to hospital. During her stay the doctors ran tests to see if there was any sign of the illness within her body. The results were negative and nothing was found. I also, of course, gave her healing but did not pick up any indication of cancer. I tried my hardest to turn her thoughts to more pleasant aspects, but to no avail. On returning to her home she was still absolutely certain that she was about to die. My poor friend soon got her wish. I had been working away for a few months and on my homecoming discovered that Ruby had again visited the hospital for further examinations. The doctors this time diagnosed cancer of the womb, which had rapidly spread into the liver. Ruby was moved into our local hospice, where she died quickly and peacefully. I loved her very dearly and would not dream of criticizing her in any way. I feel that this may have been a test that Ruby had to undergo within her lifespan. It could well have been that her soul was filtering through the vision of death into her consciousness. Whatever the reason, I know she is at peace now.

It was whilst I was training as a probationary healer that I discovered, with great humility, that I had been given a wonderful gift. I had acquired the ability to take away pain. To my delight I found that in a lot of instances headaches and backaches etc. would disappear under my touch. I had particular success at the clinic with patients suffering from migraine. I found that arthritic joints would become less painful and in some cases the throbbing sensation in the limbs would completely vanish. Somebody said to me that it was like taking an aspirin or having an injection: the ache would slowly melt away.

Norman, who had been a merchant seaman, arrived for our help one Monday evening. He sat in front of me and explained that he had been in constant agony for twenty years, ever since he had hurt his back whilst on board ship. A specialist had told him that two of the discs towards the base of the spine were causing all the trouble. He had had treatment over the years, which had obviously not been successful. I worked on him for twenty minutes and then asked him how he was feeling. He got up off the chair, stretched and moved himself backwards and forwards. With a look of amazement he turned to me and said 'The pain has gone! It's astonishing! Whilst your hands were moving up and down my spine it was as if a red-hot poker was travelling with you.'

As far as I know, he has never had any more problems with his vertebrae. It was one of those cases where a cure was instantly effected, having occurred at soul level. It is those wonderful events that make healing so worthwhile. I wish I could cure all mankind of their misery but that day is far in the distance. I only hope this book will help to bring about a more positive approach to the problems of dis-ease.

Whilst dealing with pain, I must share with my readers a method of control that was given to me by my friends in spirit. I was suffering from an inflamed abscess on one of my back teeth. The tooth was raging and I felt like banging my head against a brick wall. At that point, a voice in my ear said, 'Sit down, relax and go into meditation.' Gratefully I tried this and soon found that I had moved upwards, through a barrier, and was looking down on my pain. When I opened my eyes I found that the ache was still there, but my mind was controlling it. I have tried this exercise with several patients who have been in screaming agony, and found it to be very effective.

I use this method of pain control when I visit the dentist and for years have never had to have an injection for a filling. The dentist, unfortunately, refuses to allow me to go without a painkiller when extracting a tooth. On one visit he was performing a deep root filling and couldn't understand why I was not begging him to stop. When I explained, he accepted fully what I had said as a friend of his practised transcendental meditation. Alternative ideas are quickly spreading into the medical profession and are no longer sneered at.

Monday nights were not always serious occasions. Many of the people who came caused great merriment, and the room would often ring with laughter. One elderly lady called Doris arrived with her right arm in a sling. She had fallen in a well-known department store and sustained a nasty fracture to her wrist. The broken bone had failed to set properly, with the result that her wrist was very sore and slightly deformed. Much to the amusement of the waiting patients she informed us in a loud voice that she only wanted the pain taken away, she didn't want her wrist to straighten, as she was in the middle of a legal battle for compensation. She felt that if she had full use of her arm her expectations of hard cash would be ruined.

Another week a middle-aged woman came into the clinic holding her head. It transpired that she was suffering a massive migraine attack. In a resounding whisper, she told all and sundry that she expected us to ease her agony, but she wished to continue having her migraine as it stopped her husband pestering her in bed. 'If he thinks my headaches are gone,' she moaned, 'he'll be all over me. There'll be no stopping him!' As my grandmother once commented, 'There's nowt so queer as folk.'

During my early years with the National Federation of Spiritual Healers I listened to many brilliantly inspired speakers and visited several wonderful healing centres. The Seeker's Trust at Addington Park near Maidstone was one venue, however, to which we returned several times. I was deeply attracted by its beauty and the air of peace and tranquillity which pervaded the grounds. The Trust was started in 1925 by Charles Simpson, who was the medium for a spirit called Dr Lascelles. Several books have been written containing the teachings of this advanced soul, and I would recommend the wisdom held within their pages to any follower of the light. Continuous prayer circles are held at Addington Park for the many varied and difficult problems which afflict mankind. It was during my first visit to this retreat that a member of the Trust told me a story about the servicemen and women who were placed in the prayer circles during the war. She was very proud of the fact that every person whose name was held in the light came home safely from duties overseas at the end of the hostilities.

The presence of angels can be sensed all over the gardens and parkland and it was here that I made the acquaintance of the 'healing tree'. This was a huge oak that stood, tall and stately, on the edge of one of the pathways. It had a reputation for aiding the suffering of anyone who placed their hands on its trunk. As I stood on the grass in the afternoon sunlight, I could see the reason for this miraculous claim. On both sides of the tree, standing like sentinels, were angelic forms. One was the tree guardian, whilst the other took on the appearance of a healing deva. Their shimmering auras enfolded the oak and a large area of the surrounding land. The grounds had been the site for ancient benedictions and were still hallowed and sacred.

Although the lectures and workshops added to my knowledge and spiritual awareness, the people who made the most impression on me at that time were Ken and Irene Harrison. I can never thank them enough for their time, patience and enlightenment, which they so willingly shared with me. Besides myself, they trained Rita Prevett, who has become a dear and treasured friend, as well as Olivier Pemberton and Bill and Barbara Bray who left Southwick very able and competent healers in the service of humanity. Ken was an expert at freeing trapped nerves and unlocking limbs with joints that had become rigid. Irene, with her gentle serenity, was heaven-sent for anyone suffering from mental disorders and disabilities.

I have received a lot of mail recently pertaining to examinations and diplomas for spiritual healers. Whilst I am aware that the public have to be protected against charlatans and imposters, I am somewhat concerned that too much emphasis will be placed upon intellectual capabilities. I have seen healers, with very little book learning, perform beautiful and loving acts of service. It is from the heart that the energy of God flows out to mankind, and I hope the day will never dawn when I have to obtain a certificate to help another person place their feet on the pathway of light.

To close this chapter, let me say that it was never God's will that we should be unhappy or sick, but it is sometimes necessary for lessons to be learnt. Sickness can be caused by mistakes we have made in past lives; 'What man sows so shall he reap' is very true. A great shift in consciousness, however, will take place during the Aquarian Age and man will rethink his origins and his God. He will learn to respect himself and the rest of creation. Truly will come to pass the old esoteric words, 'Man know thyself and thou shalt know God.' The golden age will have dawned.

THE LOTUS FLOWER

Once again, sit in a comfortable upright position, close your eyes, relax and breathe a little more deeply.

See, in your mind's eye, a beautiful green field stretching out in front of you. It is a glorious summer day. The sky is a deep shade of blue and the warmth of the sun is pouring down upon you. You are without shoes and as you step into this field feel the grass beneath your feet and in between your toes. Become aware of the hum of the bees as they collect the pollen from the many varieties of wild flowers which include cowslips, daisies and buttercups. See the black and white cows feeding on the meadow, then raising their heads to regard you with their large gentle brown eyes.

Across the field you will see a stream with weeping willows growing on either side. Make your way towards this ribbon of water and stand on the bank. Did you see that quick flash of blue as the kingfisher dived past you into the brook, or the colours of the butterfly that has just landed beside you? The little river is quite shallow and as you look into the waters you will see the shapes of small fish and water insects.

Your walk takes you along the bank, between the trees, until the stream broadens out and you find yourself on the edge of a large lake. The waters appear to be almost sea-green in colour and are reflecting the circle of trees around the perimeter. As you gaze across to the other side, you see that the surface is ruffled with small ripples lapping at the edges. The more you look into the waters, the more you sense the intense peace of this enchanted place. As you feel this harmony spreading throughout your whole body, so the surface of the lake becomes still and is as smooth as glass. All is love, all is tranquil, all is calm and serene.

If you glance down at your feet you will see a small boat. As you step into this craft it moves silently away from the bank and glides smoothly across the lake. Put your hand into the water and feel your fingers trailing along beside your boat. Cup your hand and bring some of this liquid up to your lips. The taste is like pure nectar, but fresh, cool and slightly sparkling. This is healing water, so feel it filling your whole body as you drink, reaching and refreshing every organ and atom of your being.

You have now reached the far shore, so you climb from your vessel and spend a few moments just quietly contemplating the wonder of nature that is all around you. You glance again at the surface of the lake and see that, within reach of you, is a magnificent white lotus flower. The purity of this bloom is almost dazzling in its splendour. As you watch it slowly begins to open to reveal a glorious golden centre. As it enlarges more and more you are aware of your own heart centre slowly expanding with love and joy. You find that you are now standing within the centre of the lotus, which gradually changes to become a golden temple. The walls are glowing and shimmering with the shades of blue and gold, which are the colours of harmony. The roof of the temple is open to the sky and as you look upwards three pure white doves of peace fly down and come to rest at your feet. Gently take one of these doves in your hands and hold it close to your heart. Once more feel your heart centre open and beat in unison with this lovely bird. Hold your hands aloft, releasing this messenger of peace and letting the waves of love from your heart fly with the dove to any country engaged in conflict. Repeat this healing ritual with the two remaining doves, so that three different areas of the world are covered by your thoughts of serenity and freedom. Rest for a while within these temple walls to gain strength and refreshment before returning to your earthly environment.

The vision before you fades and you find yourself once more looking at the open lotus blossom floating near your feet. Beside you is the boat waiting to take you back across the large lake and into the summer meadow. Take this journey slowly, in your own time, breathing in the fresh warm air and listening to the song of the birds.

When you have walked through the meadow, gently come back to your chair, feel the seat beneath you and the floor under your feet. Within your heart retain the deep, deep peace which radiated from you out into the world. It is the peace which passeth all understanding. Before you open your eyes, see yourself enfolded within a cross of light in a circle of light.

May joy reign within your heart.

FOOTSTEP 3

Experiences as a Healer

Of all the spiritual gifts I believe healing to be
the most beautiful and rewarding. It brings with it
immense joy and love but at the same time a deep
humility. It is quite true that as you give, so shall
you receive. People ask why I do not charge money
for healing. My reply is that I am very fortunate, I
have been given boundless energy; I get back far more
than I give out; I am surrounded in light and love.
I have a wonderful family and many, many friends.
When I am in trouble there is always someone who
will offer help and sympathy.

Some of you reading this book may want to
pursue this work, so I must impress upon you the fact
that healers have a great responsibility. As the power
within us becomes stronger and brighter, we begin to
shine with an inner and outer light. I liken this to
an electric light bulb which is permanently plugged
in. People are drawn to us. On buses and trains, for
example, troubled souls will sit beside us and pour

out all their sorrows and woes. 'I don't know why I am telling you this,' they will say, but the light we give out is there for all humanity and attracts those in need. Even if we ourselves are having a bad day we must always listen and enfold that being in light and love. We will never know the outcome, but be assured that not one speck of light is ever wasted and one positive thought is worth more than a hundred negative ones. I remember getting on a bus and being confronted by a driver who had obviously got out of bed on the wrong side. He shouted and snapped at every person who tried to give him money for their fare. I spent the whole of my half-an-hour bus ride holding him in the light and by the time I reached my stop he was smiling and obviously enjoying his morning. Had I responded to him with a sharp retort his whole day would have been spent in gloom, which would have rubbed off on anybody who had the misfortune to cross his path.

It must never be forgotten that we ourselves can do nothing; we are but channels for the healing power to flow through. But as channels we can make sure that we are 'watertight'. As healers our bodies can be compared to a water jug. If the jug is dirty and cracked then the water will flow out and most of it will be lost. So, too, with healing energy. There is much we can do to make ourselves worthy of this great gift. Our bodies are temples for our spirit and like Solomon's Temple, should be worked on. We should be like the three wise monkeys: 'see no evil, hear no evil, speak no evil'. We should be kindly and loving, breathing God's fresh air, eating pure food as often as possible and exercising the mind and body. In other words be free of dis-ease. Like the good old

54

English oak tree our branches, or arms, should reach up to the heavens whilst our roots, or feet, are firmly planted in the earth.

The above advice should also be given to our patients. The stress of living in this era is enormous. The spiritual energies flowing to us as we shift into the Aquarian Age cannot always be absorbed and much of humanity is plagued by worry and over-stimulation of their mental faculties. A large percentage of man's ills can be attributed to pressure and the inability to relax.

There are several ways we can counteract this, one of them being the art of meditation. I have seen so many people benefit from this practice that I should like to see it taught as part of the educational system. Another way to combat stress is with laughter. What an important part comedy plays on this Earth. To be able to laugh without malice during these troubled years is to bring fun and pleasure. This morning, I heard on television that the first 'Laughter Clinic' has been set up under the National Health Service, to teach patients not to take life quite so seriously. Often people arrive on my doorstep, their faces pinched and frowning, with lines of stress running down from the corners of their mouths. They look lost and immensely weary. Together with counselling and healing, I try at least to make them smile. Sometimes they are able to really laugh and you see the tension begin to ebb away. They leave my front door with their faces happier and looking much more relaxed. It is also very important to be able to laugh gently at oneself. Laughter leads to positive thoughts rather than negative ones, and the body responds. The shoulders become more upright and the whole stature straightens. The sun shines once more.

This brings to mind a young man called David who came to the clinic for healing one Monday night. He had suffered for years from phobias and had been in and out of institutions for most of his adult life. David could never leave his home without going back at least a dozen times to see if he had switched the gas off or left the water tap running etc. etc. He was also terrified that he would do harm in some way to the people he came in contact with. This left him with no job, no friends and no hope.

He came for healing for about nine months. I tried to lighten his outlook but every time he sat down he said the same thing, 'This is not helping at all, but I have come just the same.' Gradually those words became, 'This is not helping at all, but I have just started a job.' Then they became, 'This is not helping at all, but I have started going out with a girl.' The last time he came to see me he said, 'This is not helping at all, I might as well be spending this half an hour playing tennis.' With great joy I sent him away to play tennis, progress with his job, love his girlfriend and get on with his life.

As part of the healing process I always give my patient a jolly good cuddle. This is because I once did this to a lady who immediately burst into tears. 'You're the first person to treat me with any affection for about ten years,' she sobbed. Some people have little physical contact with other human beings and with our English tradition of the stiff upper lip we are afraid to touch in case of ridicule. What a great pity; what a difference a good hug would make to all our lives. Love does indeed make the world go round.

How I would like to say to the newspapers, 'Let's have one day a week when every item of reporting is on positive, cheerful events.' How I would like to see television presenting a programme that taught viewers how to use love and light for their own happiness as well as helping to heal the world of its many problems. If people worked nationwide and worldwide, through the media, what a vision of hope would shine forth as we entered the Aquarian Age.

Healing energy works in many different ways. Over the years I have seen some 'instant miracles' where a back, a limb or a situation responds immediately, but usually it would take more than one visit and I have come to the conclusion that true healing, which lasts, has to come from soul level. A patient's whole attitude, his approach to life, his very thinking has to change. Sometimes what a patient has believed for a whole lifetime is shaken up and he finds he is looking in an entirely different direction. Rigidity of mind can cause many dis-eases of the body. In the Aquarian Age the mind will become very important and we have to learn to use our thoughts so that they flow in harmony with our physical bodies. Healers, in particular, must always be aware of the strength of their own thinking. Our minds are becoming very potent and any negativity or dark reflections will have twice the force and power of that of the average man with no spiritual knowledge.

I remember one lady, called Mary, very well. She came to us for healing only once. She arrived very agitated and appeared at her wit's end. She sat down with the words, 'You are my only hope. If you can't help me, I shall end it all.' She was in her late forties and during her teenage years had done 'something dreadful'. What this 'something' was we never heard, but for years this had played on her mind and had become an obsession. She had just been married for the second time and was enjoying a happy loving relationship. However, what she had done in her teens was eating more and more into her waking hours. She wanted to tell her new husband about it, but was frightened of his reaction and found that she couldn't speak of it. We gave her healing and she left.

We didn't see or hear any more from her until about a month later when she appeared again. 'I haven't come for healing,' she said, 'only to thank you.' It turned out that she had gone straight home from the clinic and immediately told her new husband her 'dreadful secret'. 'So what?' he said. 'Many people have done that – what's all the fuss about?' Her mind was free and she was a very happy lady. The healing had given her courage, a change of attitude and peace of mind.

A lot of people, particularly men, were very sceptical when they arrived at the clinic. This was the attitude of a patient called Arthur when he first visited us. He could hardly walk and was helped into the room by a friend. He plonked himself down on the chair with the words, 'I don't believe any of this rubbish, but you are my last resort.' A diabetic, Arthur was on large doses of insulin, which had eaten into his bones. The pain was unbearable and he would soon be confined to a wheelchair. The medical profession could do nothing more to help him.

He came to us regularly every Monday over the next six months, and his condition slowly improved until he was walking unaided. He then went for a blood test and to his amazement the hospital found his blood to be almost back to normal. With his progress back to health came the questions, 'Where does the healing come from?' 'Is there really such a thing as God?' His mind became open to new ideas, his life took on new meaning. His healing had truly been from soul level. When he stopped coming to see us, he was well enough to go back to work and with a friend had opened up a new business. He was still a diabetic, but it was under control.

I have always been intensely interested in the many different methods of healing and it was whilst I was working with the National Federation of Spiritual Healing that I found one that was to take my feet up another step on the path of light. I went to a lecture entitled 'New Age Healing' by an inspired lady called Brenda Johnston. We were so impressed that for the next year my friend Rita Prevett and I travelled to Havant once a fortnight to study this particular procedure.

Brenda is a member of the Arcane School, which arises from the teachings of Alice Bailey and the Tibetan Master, and has developed a method of healing in the energy field via the etheric body. Every living creature, plant and tree on this planet has an etheric body surrounding the physical frame. It is our individual energy field and without it we couldn't function. We wouldn't be able to assimilate and expel food, walk, think or speak. In fact we would be lifeless. All disease which manifests in the physical body must first appear in the etheric. Using this method of healing, signs of disease can be detected before reaching our dense body. If the etheric is healthy, so is the physical.

The etheric field is composed of lines of energy in constant motion. Where these lines cross are located chakras, which are spiritual openings linking the etheric body to the physical frame. There are seven major centres located between the top of our head and the base of the spine, linked to and controlling the major glands of the endocrine system of our bodies.

Brenda taught us to pick up and feel the energy flowing through these centres, with our fingertips. She taught us how to balance these energies so that all the chakras were brought into harmony with the major glands, thereby vitalizing the physical organs connected to those glands. She taught us how to feel all the organs of the body, tracing the intestines and the spinal cord etc., enabling us to feel and pick up trouble within the etheric field before it manifested in the dense body.

Brenda Johnston and her international team of tutors, including medical doctors, have now formed a charity called the International Network for Esoteric Healing (previously International Health Research Network). This method of healing is now taught in twenty-one countries and several doctors are offering four courses in America, including one at a medical school as an optional extra.

This was a time of great learning, of working on another level of consciousness. I became aware of the importance of our etheric, astral, mental and spiritual bodies and how much they affected the health and well-being of all of us. For instance, feelings of anger, greed, envy, fear etc. cause disharmony within the astral or feeling body, which is reflected through the solar plexus centre into the physical frame. The same thing applies within the mental field where negative and perverse attitudes are mirrored through the throat centre and again enter the dense body. It is just like a chain reaction from one level of consciousness to another. On the other hand, if we think positively and surround ourselves with love and light, what a difference it makes to our health and fitness. Our energy field looks brighter and our chakras become more balanced.

Since those days of tuition from Brenda I have taken this form of healing and adapted it to my own use with extremely good results. This is truly a method of healing from the soul, a method that will take us into the Aquarian Age and beyond. I am sure that mankind and our planet Earth are moving very quickly towards that golden age when the very atoms of our bodies will be filled with light and the denseness of solid matter will be just a memory.

Over the years I have discovered that this healing approach is very beneficial for patients who are spiritually aware. It is surprising how many of them say to me, 'I can feel exactly where you are with your fingers and what you are doing', although my hands are usually about six to nine inches away from their bodies. A friend who is a gifted astrologer came to see me last year for this form of treatment. She was experiencing a lot of trouble with her throat and the hospital had found a small growth, which was naturally causing her some concern. As I was working, she was able to tell me precisely what was happening and when she felt in harmony with the flow of energy. After several visits she returned to the hospital for more tests and the doctors were unable to explain what had happened to the growth or where it had gone. She is still having treatment for other problems on her throat but at least the worry of the growth has left her. Once several years ago, when I was working on her spine, using on the body methods, she suddenly said she felt as if she was on fire. The heat was pouring up her spine and spreading to all her limbs; she said she felt like a volcano. After she had cooled down the pain in her back had gone and the healing had been successful.

No chapter on healing could be written without mentioning the animal kingdom, although I have devoted a larger section to them later on in this book. I have loved animals all my life, long before I learnt to love people, and could talk for hours on the cats I have owned. Animals are a joy to work with; they are incapable of erecting any form of barrier or blockage, unlike humans. Their response to the energy is a delight to feel. They are still so pure that the angels have little difficulty in drawing close and performing their healing tasks. I have recently been seeing a golden retriever called Ben. As soon as I ring the bell and he sees me on his doorstep, he takes himself off and positions himself in the lounge in exactly the same spot where I give him healing every week. He enjoys my weekly visits and turns his body this way and that so that I can easily get to all the parts that are causing him trouble.

Animals will give their love to you regardless of colour or creed. They don't care if you are ugly, fat, black, white or even if you have two heads. What a pity the human race doesn't follow their lead. When

I worked at the clinic I saw an enormous amount of pain and stress caused by relationships between individuals, either inside the marriage or without. Several times I have just given the advice, 'Go home and love your other half.' Apart from healing, we are often called upon to act as Marriage Guidance Counsellors and Samaritans rolled into one. Strangers will frequently tell you things that they wouldn't tell anyone close to them. Many times I pick up the telephone and spend the next hour listening to someone I will never meet unburden themselves. I say very little; I just let them talk, which helps them to release negative energy. It is all part of the healing process. Usually they will finish their conversation with the words, 'Thank you so much for letting me talk. I feel much better now. I really am quite calm.'

One day a very nervous man arrived for healing at the clinic. He had obviously had a drink to give himself some courage and, swaying slightly, he sat down on the chair in front of me. He explained very timidly that he never had any luck with dating the members of the female sex. It transpired that he was impotent. A humorous thought popped into my head as to where I should put my hands. I calmed him down and gave him general healing, hoping that the angels would provide an answer for him. He didn't come back for any more treatment, but a few months later I saw him walking arm in arm with a young man. I felt his problem had been solved and in my heart wished him every happiness. Does it really matter how or where we give affection as long as we truly love?

Drink and drug victims would also arrive on Monday nights and over the years I have come into frequent contact with these unhappy souls. I once more run a healing clinic, this time in Brighton, and am finding drugs to be a very grave problem. Just recently a young man arrived to see me. He was well-educated and had a very good job in the Brighton area. The problem was, however, that in the evenings he got bored and had enough money to visit the night clubs and discos that abound in this section of Sussex. He had made a new set of friends who were heavily into the so-called 'soft' drugs. He had experimented and found them to be very exciting. He had felt good and on his 'trips' saw wonderful places with his inner vision. One evening, about two months before he came to see me, his friends had persuaded him to try LSD. He immediately began to tremble and spent the worst night of his life. He saw horrific images and had the most dreadful feelings of fear and panic. It took him two days to recover from the drug, which had left him depressed, withdrawn and still filled with fear. Instead of getting better, these emotions were getting worse. I started working on him and found that his etheric body had completely shifted. It was, in fact, standing beside his physical frame instead of round it. I was surprised that he was functioning at all. It took several visits but I eventually managed to ease it back into place and slowly he began to return to normal. Even after the shock he had had, he still wanted to know if it would be all right for him to take 'soft' drugs again. I explained that his energy field would be weak for a very long while and any more drug-taking would probably kill him. I advised him to take up meditation when he felt stronger, which would give the same 'lift' without the dangers. What I didn't tell him was that the LSD had also brought him into contact with the lower astral plane and hence the black images which he had glimpsed. The same thing happens to alcoholics when they shake with the DTs and see spiders climbing up the walls; their etheric field becomes very loose and out of place.

Two diseases that we never came into contact with at the Southwick clinic were Aids and ME, both of which have appeared within the last ten years, and involve a broken-down immune system that causes the patient to become prone to other ailments. Again, it is the etheric body that we should be looking at. I have found that in both illnesses the etheric body has become very weak with little energy flowing through the chakras. After balancing and working to strengthen this field, patients have reported that they feel less tired and more able to cope with their difficulties.

I have spent about twenty years now acting as a channel for healing and during that time I have heard many sad and dreadful stories. Very little can surprise or shock me now about human acts, some wonderful, others horrific. What I have developed, however, is a deep and abiding love for humanity, warts and all. Under all the dross, there is a great brightness waiting to expand and shine throughout the universe. Mankind will win through and one day our planet and the people who inhabit it will become sacred and take their rightful places as Lords and leaders in God's great plan for our solar system and beyond.

THE HEALING TEMPLE

As in previous meditations, close your eyes and relax as much as possible. Breathe a little bit deeper and begin to feel that you are wrapped in a warm soft cloak. This cloak represents pure love. It is enfolding you and raising you in consciousness into the world of light, the world of spirit.

Using your inner vision you will find yourself in a beautiful rose garden. It is a warm summer's day with a gentle breeze blowing, bringing to you the perfume of the roses. Walk around the garden for a little while, stopping to admire the many different coloured blooms. You are drawn to a rose of a particular hue; stop and gaze at the wonder of its creation. Look at the formation of the petals, the way the centre is gently curved to protect the heart of the flower. On one of the petals is a droplet of water, which is reflecting the pure and gentle radiance of the flower. The colour you have chosen has a special meaning just for you. Meditate on this and you will receive the benefit of the qualities of that individual rose. Without picking the flower, hold its image against your heart. Feel the rose opening as your heart centre expands, sending waves of love to all creation living in the physical world.

In the centre of the garden you will see a magnificent temple. It is circular in shape with the roof open to the sky. The walls are shimmering with light giving an iridescent image of many different colours. There are two large pillars at the front of the temple, with wide steps running up to them. At the top of the slope you see a figure clothed in white with his hands outstretched in welcome. He bids you climb the steps and enter the temple beside him. This is one of the many healing centres in the world of spirit and as you walk in between the pillars you are aware of a feeling of intense love and peace flooding through your whole body.

The inside of the temple appears to be lit with a pure blue light that is pouring through the open roof. Around the walls you will notice seven stained-glass windows through which are reflected the seven colours of the spectrum. Under these windows are positioned low comfortable couches, upon which are reclining the patients who have been brought here for healing. Never forget that you can come back here any time you wish and bring with you anyone who is in need of the calming rays. Behind the couches, under the stained-glass windows, are seven great angels of healing, directing the colours down onto their sick patients. In the centre of the temple is an altar made of pure crystal, which is glowing with light. Behind the altar appears the great healer himself, the Master Jesus. His hands are raised in blessing and as you look into his eyes you see that they are filled with a deep love and compassion. He knows all your troubles and your problems. Always remember that you are never alone; he is always waiting to give strength and comfort. If you wish, lie down on one of the couches and ask that help be given to you. You may just prefer to sit and be filled with love and light, pouring healing from your own heart to all the suffering people of the world or anyone you know personally to be in trouble.

When you are ready to leave, climb down the steps and find yourself once more in the rose garden.

Spend just a short time walking on the grass between the bushes. Listen to the birds and watch the bees collecting nectar from the flowers.

With reluctance, it is time to depart and you see in front of you a pathway leading through a gateway and out of the garden. As you walk down this path you are slowly lowering your vibrations until you find yourself back in your chair and in your familiar surroundings. Just stretch your arms and feel your feet on the ground. Imagine yourself wrapped in a cloak of light and protection. You are once more ready to face the world, filled with healing love and peace that will give you strength to face any worries in the coming days or weeks.

FOOTSTEP 4

Through Darkness Into Light

I pondered long and hard before including this chapter in my book. I was urged very strongly, however, by the Masters and my friends in spirit, to put these experiences into words. The episode that I am about to share with you was the most glorious and, at the same time, the most terrifying of my life. The darkness and the light came together to show me that they are both two sides of the same coin, and that all occurrences are part of God's perception. It is true that every hair of our heads is numbered and not a sparrow falls that he does not know about. We all live and endure within that omnipotent power we call God.

At some point on the spiritual path, we have to meet and conquer what is known as 'The Dweller on the Threshold'. This being, or entity, is the sum total of all the negative deeds that we have performed during our many lives and every act of suffering that we have caused is built into this shadow. In one of our incarnations, when we feel strong enough, we have to face this vision of darkness of our own making. This, then, is the story of my encounter with my own personal 'Dweller on the Threshold'.

I remember very clearly how it started, about fourteen years ago. I was suffering from a heavy cold and was at home recuperating. I had in those days a very beautiful and much-loved black-and-white cat called Willum. We were both in the lounge, enjoying each other's company, when the programme I was watching on the television came to an end. I switched off the set and turned to look at my companion. To my horror, instead of Willum, I was confronted by a hideous black form with eye sockets, but no eyes. At the same time I experienced a shock to my solar plexus of utter fear. I shook my head and everything returned to normal. Over the next few weeks, however, the visions of these unspeakable thought-forms got worse and worse. The waves of terror to my solar plexus were constant and dreadful. At first I thought I was going mad and told no-one. I felt better when I was out in the open air, so spent most of my days walking in the country or over the downlands. I couldn't confide in my husband; he would never have understood and would have insisted that I seek psychiatric help. I began to realize, with consternation, that I was under some sort of psychic attack. I was panic-stricken.

The bombardment continued getting stronger and stronger. I was aware that the entity was growing larger and larger as it fed upon my fear. Slowly I came to the conclusion that it was personal to me; it had not been sent by anybody else. I knew that I had to deal with it myself, to overcome it on my own. I was conscious that all my friends in spirit were standing back and were not allowed to help me. It was as if they were saying, 'We are so sorry, but you must meet and overpower this darkness by yourself.'

I then decided to seek advice and went to everyone and everywhere for assistance. I cowered in Ken's and Irene's house and telephoned anyone I thought might aid me. I prayed at my sister's grave and sat for hours in various churches. I was given lots of different words of wisdom – sit in a pyramid of protection, shoot it down with shafts of light, do this, do that – nothing lessened the power of that evil image by one inch. It overshadowed me with its negativity and no action of mine would make it remove its talons from my consciousness.

I couldn't eat, I couldn't sleep and I was losing so much weight that even my husband was beginning to get suspicious. One Sunday morning Peter found me in tears and demanded to know what was the matter with me. I longed to confide in him but I found enough strength to smile and say, 'It's all right dear, I've just been overworking.' I was at the end of my tether, but that very night there was an intervention from the brothers of light.

For several evenings I had been shocked to find that this dark force had changed its tactics. It was now trying to get into my mind. I knew that if it succeeded it would mean the end of my mental stability for this lifetime. I had also recognized what I was dealing with and that it was, indeed, 'The Dweller on the Threshold'. I couldn't cope with it and I didn't know how to. This particular night, I had gone to bed very late and was lying awake with Peter asleep beside me. It was about two o'clock in the morning when the now familiar shock waves started their attack. The darkness came and began to overshadow my mind. I could hold out no longer.

From deep within my being, from the depths of my soul, I silently screamed for the 'Christ'. How can I possibly put into words what happened next! My bedroom filled with golden light. I experienced the most intense and profound love, the depth of which I may never encounter again. It surrounded and filled me, it entered my body and I became at one with the light and love. I was all light; I was all love; I was part of God at the highest level. The evil had evaporated; there was no past or future, only NOW and a feeling of sublime wonder and a deep, deep, peace. The golden light had become the figure of a man, who in later years I was to recognize as the Lord Maitreya, God's representative of the Christ light on earth.

I don't know how long it was before the figure of this Master faded and the light slowly melted away. It could have been an hour, it could have been only seconds; time had stood still but the whole of eternity had entered my room. I must have fallen happily asleep for my next memory was of finding myself in a garden filled with flowers, birds and animals. I was met by a monk in a brown habit, beloved St Francis, and for the rest of that night I was given the freedom of his beautiful garden in the realms of spirit.

When I awoke next morning, I wish I could have said that the entity had completely disappeared. It was still there, but not so forceful and never again, in the days ahead, did it try to overpower my mind.

It was, however, my dark night of the soul, so I would have to vanquish it. I knew that I could now tackle this task with renewed strength and vigour, for I had been given the key. It was, as always, so simple, just pure love. I turned and faced my 'Dweller' with joy and total forgiveness of self. This is so important, that you are able to absolve yourself for all the unhappiness and pain that you have caused. So slowly, with love over the next few weeks, I dissolved my own dark image, my own dark mirror. The thought-forms were transmuted and where there had been negative energy, now lived only light and illumination.

I hope that this story will not frighten or discourage any reader. Your experience, when it comes, will be entirely different to mine. It may well have already happened in another incarnation. Your 'Dweller' will probably be much easier to shift than mine but I have given you the passwords 'love and compassion'. I can only add that from that night onwards, the energy we know as God's light became a part of my everyday living. I feel very humble that I was allowed to undertake that initiation in this lifetime. It taught me a great deal and allowed me to take a large stride on my evolutionary path.

It wasn't long before I was again called to assist in the removing of negative influences. A close friend rang me one evening and asked if I could do something to help a colleague where she worked. It transpired that this lady, whom we shall call Iris, was married to a man who was dabbling with the darker side of the occult. He had joined a group who were using spiritual energy for their own self-gratification and to influence the minds of other human beings. To be very kind to them, we shall call them 'grey'.

73

Iris was very worried because her husband had started to change in a very extraordinary way. He kept telling her that he was changing into a wolf and had become very hysterical and frantic. Iris assured my friend that some of what her husband was saying was true. She herself had seen hair growing on his hands and his facial features become more pointed and pronounced. She had also heard strange noises that she could only describe as howls coming from their bedroom. She was very concerned that their only child would become affected.

I called upon the help of two friends and together we joined hands, sat in a circle and asked the brotherhood of light to rescue this man from his own foolishness. A few days later I had a call to say that Iris was pleased and delighted. She had gone to bed on the night of our intervention, fallen asleep and experienced a very clear dream. She said that she had seen three women sitting in a circle and described our hair colouring and what clothes we were wearing. She was very accurate in her account and I must add that she had never met me, so she didn't know what I looked like. She finished by saying that her dream ended with the sound of a wolf howling, which got softer and softer as it disappeared into the distance. She later telephoned to say that her husband was back to normal. I only hope that he learnt from his stupidity and ceased meddling with forces he could not control.

As illustrated above, there are grave dangers lurking for the man who thinks he can gain power through the use of negative energy. I have come across several sad souls who have experimented with the Ouija board and have drawn towards themselves an inhabitant from the lower astral plane. Quite a few beds in our mental hospitals are taken up by patients who are deranged as a result of their brush with spiteful entities. A wise teacher once taught me that balance, on the spiritual path, is like a three-legged stool. She said you must practise three virtues – the gaining of wisdom that has to be shared, meditation from the heart and service to all creation. By following these three maxims, no harm can befall any follower on the path of light.

I have come to understand that no evil originates from God, only from man himself. There are dark angels as well as light angels and it is the dark messengers who bring to us our lessons. Much nonsense is talked about Lucifer, or the devil, as most people call him. At the dawn of creation, he was one of God's highest ambassadors. It is said that he sat at the right-hand side of God. When man had reached the point, in his early development, when it was time for him to become individualized and start to reason, God had a problem. Man was given free will and was allowed to make his own decisions, for good or bad. God required someone to take on the burdens of mankind and bring to them the negative lessons needed for their evolution. Lucifer volunteered to make this supreme sacrifice because of his love for humanity. He left his exalted position and, drawing near to mankind, set up his kingdom on the astral plane. Here he has laboured unceasingly for the benefit of the human race. His army of dark angels has brought to this planet some very painful but necessary lessons. It is interesting to note that we often call him Satan and it is through the influences of the planet Saturn that most of our negative experiences arrive. Just for a moment pause and consider what a commitment this superior angel has made. He has had to spend thousands of years being reviled, cursed and misunderstood by the very people he has such an affection for. If you look back on your own life, you will realize that it is through the mistakes you have made that you have gained wisdom and progressed. When humanity has at last reached the stage in its evolution when Lucifer is no longer required, he will return to his spiritual home and take up his rightful place again by the side of God. Lucifer, the fallen angel, never fell from the grace of God; he just lowered his vibrations to allow himself to work close to the earth plane. It is man who has caused such darkness, in his name, by forming satanic groups and enacting fearful rituals in order to gain power and wealth.

As I have just mentioned, all the evil in the world has been caused by the acts of mankind. Thoughts are particles of living energy which build into thought-forms. When these feelings are malicious and depraved, they become entities of great strength that feed on the fear of countries or people. You have only to reflect on the years of Nazi rule in Germany to understand what a hypnotic effect the evil thought-forms had on the population of that country. That is what happened in former Yugoslavia, with neighbour killing neighbour. You will realize, therefore, how important it is to build positive thought-forms. Love is the sword that must be used to cut through the gloom surrounding this earth. Man has caused the chaos, so man must be responsible for its ultimate clearance.

As I have already said, a thought-form is a living

structure of energy and it is these forms which often cause problems within houses and old buildings. They are shadows of past events, where passionate thoughts of intense negativity have formed. This is why homes where murders have been committed are seen to have 'ghosts', which take on the appearance of the killer or his victim. The perpetuator of this evil and the casualty of his crime will often, themselves, be drawn back to the horrific scene. Once trapped within the darkness, the murderer is unable to leave until he has repented for his outrage and asked forgiveness of his victim. I am not an expert in this area of psychic phenomena, but there are a number of good, strong spiritual men and women who can perform the ceremony of exorcism necessary to free these buildings from evil.

Joan Fugeman, a kindred soul and close friend, and I were recently asked if we would go and try to help a lady who lived in a house within our local area. This woman, who was in poor health herself, could sense a dark image in certain parts of the home. She also said that she was aware of the smell of rotten vegetables, which made me very suspicious. Joan and I wandered about the various rooms; we both felt that the back bedroom was the main area for negative vibrations. We joined hands and sat in silent prayer and meditation. We asked the White Brotherhood, who watch over mankind, to come and bring the light of Christ into the room. We asked that they either dissolve the thought-form or, if it was an entity, take it up into the light of God and free it from the bonds of this earth. On completing our prayer for deliverance and leaving the bedroom, we discovered that we had both sensed the same apparition. We had seen a monk in a dark habit with the cowl pulled down over his face. I had felt that this was a strong thought-form of a very unhappy man. It appeared to me that the figure had been trapped in a monastic life to which he was totally unsuited. He could not cope with the rigid restrictions and enforced celibacy, with the result that he had become totally deranged. The thought-form he had left, on death, was very strong and had lingered over the centuries. When questioned, the lady of the house gave us the information that the land had once been part of a monastery. I understand that she had no further problems and the house returned to normal.

This was a fairly mild experience, unlike another occasion when Joan and I were called to a large bungalow where feelings of intense darkness were being encountered. This time we noticed the waves of blackness as soon as we entered the building. In the front room we both felt the hairs on the back of our necks stand up and it needed all our reserves of strength not to turn and run. Once again, we linked hands and called upon the help of the Brotherhood of Light. We became channels for the pure white light of love which flows from the heart of God. We flooded and poured this love through every room, sweeping away all the evil influences from our path. When we had finished our task, we went out into the sunlit garden where the tenant of the bungalow was waiting. He told us that whilst we had been working, the front door of the dwelling had burst open and he had seen the dark shape of a man with a large black dog rush from the building. As I have said before, nothing can stand up to the power of love.

Quite often, I will go into a house and sense that all

is not well within the family. Maybe there have been rows or shouting, or perhaps their thoughts have not been harmonious. Some blame for this must lie with the programmes on television. Every night we view mayhem and violence, which is served up to us in the name of enjoyment. Think how much better our thought-forms would be within our home if what we saw was really family entertainment. How much more beneficial it would be if our viewing produced agreeable thoughts and our dreams at night were not tinged by the traumatic visions we watch on our screens.

As a conclusion to this chapter, I feel that I must just touch on the subject of suicide. Sometimes, troubled patients will ask me about their loved ones who committed suicide: what happened to them after they died; have they gone across properly; are they still terribly unhappy?

A lot of nonsense is talked about these dejected souls who choose to self-destruct. We are told that they are left, unaided and unloved, to roam the realms of the astral until it is time for them to reincarnate. The Roman Catholic Church used to bury suicide victims in unconsecrated ground as an act of punishment. What utter rubbish! My God is a god of love and compassion, who is all understanding and all wise. He cherishes us, he does not condemn us for failure. He helps us to pick ourselves up and try again. My belief is that people who commit suicide are met at death, taken through the tunnel of light, and treated with much love and sympathy by caring, spiritual beings who have chosen to do that work. They are helped to come to terms with their sorrow and travel the same road after death as the rest of us. At some point on their journey they have to come to terms with their inability to continue that past life. In a future reincarnation they will be required to meet the same test again and hopefully have enough strength to overcome their weaknesses. I think we have all had a life when this has happened to us, so we should never judge or criticize another person's misfortune.

People who contemplate suicide have reached a point where they have become obsessed with their own failures. They are always extremely negative and, therefore, attract towards themselves thought-forms of similar darkness. These forms build and build, until the poor sufferer is too weak to resist and terminates his own life. A friendly face or a kind voice could have made all the difference and would have broken the chain of dissenting thoughts. This is one of the reasons why the Samaritans perform such a wonderful service; they are always there when needed and are only a telephone call away.

Like most healers, I have patients who are contemplating suicide. I always encourage them to ring me when they are feeling particularly low at any time of the day or night. I was especially glad that I once said this to a young woman who was going through a bad patch, and threatening to kill herself. She rang me at two-thirty one morning from a telephone kiosk. She could hardly speak, her words were slurred and her conversation made little sense. As her tone grew weaker and weaker, I was able to find out that she was calling me from her local public phonebox. I quickly contacted the police and rang for an ambulance. With my husband driving, we raced to the location where I knew her to be. When we arrived she had already been taken to hospital, where they managed to save her life. She is now happy and contented, with everything to live for.

I trust that this chapter has not made anyone feel gloomy. I hope you will see the light and love shining through every page and realize that nothing is ever hopeless once you put your feet on the path. With assistance from the dark angels, I took some very large steps forward on my spiritual journey.

STEPPING STONES AND BOULDERS

As you gently relax in your chair, breathing a little more deeply, you become aware that your guardian angel is behind you. She is wrapping you softly in her wings of light and raising you in consciousness into the spiritual world.

You find yourself looking across a small picturesque valley, towards a lake that is glistening in the sunlight. There is a pathway running between fields of ripe yellow corn, swaying in the breeze, forming waves of undulating glory. As you walk along this narrow road between the golden pastures, your mood lifts and you feel light-hearted and full of good humour. The birds are singing their praises and the sunshine is pouring down upon you, bringing warmth and healing. 'God's in his heaven, all's right with the world.'

The lake in the distance draws nearer, and you see that at the far end a waterfall cascades down from some rocks jutting out from the side of a hill. For a while just sit and gaze at the beauty of the scene and watch the water falling into the pool, causing ripples to flow across the whole surface of the lake. You will notice that there are seven stepping stones forming a walkway across to the bank on the other side. Each stone represents a spiritual aspiration, so as you step onto the first one, let the essence of its teaching be absorbed into your awareness. The seven stepping stones contain the following disciplines:

1. Purity of thought – feel love for all humanity without criticism or censure. Let these blameless thoughts surround the whole earth, cleansing and healing.

2. Wisdom – let this enlightenment flow from your heart to all the leaders and statesmen of every country on earth, bringing freedom to all men.

3. Power – let spiritual strength flow out to all leaders and statesmen, so that truth may be upheld.

4. Forgiveness – ask for compassion and pardon for all the evil in the world, that it may be transmuted into love.

5. Healing – surround the earth in the restorative colour of gold, asking that the ozone layer may be revitalized.

6. Positivity – pray that the thoughts of all people on earth may become beneficial and constructive.

7. Love – from your heart pour out this benediction to all creation and to the earth itself.

You are now on the far side of the lake, standing next to the waterfall. As you watch this sheet of pure water falling into the lake, you see that all the colours of the rainbow are contained within its structure. Step under this natural shower and let the healing shades pour over you, refreshing and purifying every atom of your being. Sit on the bank for a short while and let the warmth of the summer day dry your body.

You turn to gaze at the hill behind the fountain of water, and observe that there is a small path running up the side. This is the next stage of your journey. The road is quite narrow and you will find it difficult to keep your feet from wandering off the path. You will also see that there are seven fairly large boulders between you and the summit of the hill. These rocks represent either people who need your forgiveness or mortals who want absolution from you.

It will take a while for you to walk this section of your meditation, but you will find that as you stop at each boulder, and pardon or accept forgiveness from the people you have named, the stone will be rolled away. You may find that you have to return to this meditation several times before you can completely clear the walkway.

Once all the obstacles have been removed, you can quickly climb the rest of the way to the top of the hill. As you stand, looking at the wonderful view on either side of you, the rays from the sun pour down upon you. This is the Christ light, from the spiritual realms, bringing you redemption and complete peace of mind. In forgiving, you are truly forgiven.

The vision fades and you find yourself once more walking between the fields of waving corn, taking the road back to where it all began. It has been a journey of understanding and fulfilment.

Breathe a little bit deeper and find that you are once more back in familiar surroundings. Imagine that your physical body is enveloped in light, which is God's protection. Open your eyes and when you are ready, leave your chair and take up your earthly duties once more.

FOOTSTEP 5

The White Eagle Lodge

After my experiences with the powers of darkness, I felt that I needed a spiritual base. This wish was soon answered and I found myself attending my first White Eagle public service.

Aunt Sheila, my friend and companion on the path, drew my attention to a notice in our local paper. It said that the White Eagle Crowborough Daughter Lodge was now holding services in Brighton on Tuesdays and Sundays. They were conducting a meeting on the following day, so we went along to find out what it was all about. The service was held in the Unitarian church, and as I walked through the door and sat down, I felt a sense of peace and quiet tranquillity. As the ceremony progressed, the faces of certain people seemed very familiar to me and I knew that I had at last 'come home'. From that day onwards the White Eagle Lodge became my spiritual family and my resting-place. For those of you who have no knowledge of this beautiful healing church,

I will try to explain how it was created and why its message of love and hope has spread into many other countries throughout the world.

The White Eagle Lodge was founded, with the encouragement of the White Brotherhood in the world of spirit, by Grace and Ivan Cooke in 1936. Grace was the medium for a very advanced guide, an Indian chief known as White Eagle. White Eagle means wise teacher, which is a very apt description as to read one of White Eagle's books, written through the mediumship of Grace, is to open a door into the wonder of other realms of life. As you digest his words, you are inspired and raised up into a higher level of consciousness. There is seldom a page of his writings that does not contain the word LOVE. His teachings are so simple, but at the same time so profound. The ancient wisdom comes alive and the purpose of existence is explained. The good and the negative events of one's life begin to make sense. You can look back into the past and see a thread running through, which has brought you to the present point in your incarnation. These teachings are the foundation and cornerstone of the Lodge. It is a place of service and healing to mankind, the four kingdoms of nature and to mother earth herself. One of the reasons why the White Eagle Lodge was brought into manifestation by the Brotherhood of Light was to help mankind to overcome the trials and difficulties that would herald the Aquarian Age. It is achieving this purpose and much more. Its light shines into the darkest regions of the earth, blessing all, condemning none, and its arms reach out to the four corners of the globe, spiritually protecting and defending the weak and helpless.

The first home for the work was at Burstow, between Brighton and London, and then at Pembroke Hall in Kensington. When Pembroke Hall was bombed out during the war, the Lodge was moved to St Mary Abbots Place, also in Kensington, which is still the home of the London Lodge today. In 1945, under White Eagle's guidance, a new property called New Lands was purchased at Liss in Hampshire. It was on this land that an exquisite domed temple was erected: a light centre that was to spread its love and influence from the heart of Britain to every living atom of God's creation. Two smaller temples of similar design have now been built at Willomee in Australia and Montgomery, Texas, in America. These form a perfect triangle of sacred perfection. A triangle is a very strong symbol of spiritual wisdom, love and power.

Grace and Ivan Cooke, their work completed, have passed peacefully into spirit. The Lodge is now in the safe hands of their daughters Joan and Ylana, who are helped by their children Jenny, Jeremy and Colum. The whole family, including husbands, wives and grandchildren, devote their lives to the continuation of the teachings. I would recommend that my readers go to a service at either Liss or London and experience for themselves the beauty and sheer magic of the vibrations from these two temples. The complete account of the formation and growth of these centres is told in the publication *The Story of the White Eagle Lodge*.

We are often led to certain situations when it is time for us to take another step upwards on our spiritual path. This happened to me just before I came into contact with White Eagle's writings. I do not astrally project or have 'out of the body experiences', but I do undergo what I call 'walk-about' dreams. I fall asleep and immediately become aware that a guide is with me. He leads me into various regions of the spirit world and stays with me. On waking, I have total recall and the memory doesn't leave me. I find that this only occurs when I need to learn something, or if I am about to take another stride on my journey into light. On this particular occasion, I went to bed early and quickly fell asleep. A friend in spirit was waiting for me, and we travelled to an area of shining radiance and glorious colour. I found myself outside a small thatched cottage, just like you see on picture postcards. The garden was full of wild flowers and it even had roses climbing round the door. I noticed that the windows were lattice-shaped, with gleaming panes of glass letting in the sunlight. I knocked on the door and it was opened by an elderly gentleman with grey hair. He had a wonderful smile and a pair of kind gentle eyes that seemed to twinkle all the time. He was dressed in rather old-fashioned clothes and was wearing a pair of brown carpet slippers. My gaze was particularly drawn to his footwear and I remember being very concerned that he did not have any shoes.

He welcomed me in and ushered me into his front room, which was very light and airy. There were two cats in a chair, one tabby and one black, who stretched themselves and lifted their heads to be stroked. I adore cats, so it made me feel very much at home. In the middle of the room, instead of a table, stood a large bagatelle board. In modern language, a pinball machine. My grey-haired friend invited me to play a game. The black and white balls used in this contest were hit with a silver stick. Some of the balls landed on high numbers, others on low numbers, whilst some rolled back to the beginning. After I had finished, my elderly gentleman told me that the bagatelle machine represented my past lives. In quite a few of my incarnations I had managed to collect high numbers, which was good, but in others I had only been able to pick up low scores. In several lives my balls had gone back to the start and I had had to do it all again.

He lifted the orbs off the board and put them back in a box which looked like a seaman's trunk. I noticed that a lot of them were white and shining but others had dark patches ingrained into them. He explained that they illustrated my soul on its path back to the godhead. I said that by the look of the grimy ones I still had a long way to travel. He laughed and put his arm round my shoulders, leading me over to the chest containing the balls. He closed the lid and showed me the top, which was covered with mother-of-pearl, all ablaze with light. It was so bright that it hurt my eyes. This, he said, was how my soul would look at the end of my journey. He had given me a view into the past and a glance into the future. I felt very humble as the Lords of Karma must have given their permission for this incident. I had been allowed a brief glimpse at the glory of my own resurrection, when my soul would merge with my spirit to become one. My elderly friend escorted me to the door of his cottage where my guide was waiting. We waved goodbye and the next thing I remember was waking up, in my physical body, ready to start a new day.

A short time after joining the Crowborough and

Brighton Daughter Lodge, I went on an evening visit to the temple at Liss. I walked in through the doors and paused at the bookstall just inside the entrance hall. Propped up at the front of the table was a picture of White Eagle. My heart nearly stopped with shock. The face I was looking at was my elderly gentleman in carpet slippers. Thank you, my wise mentor. I know that with your help I will one day reach the summit and an even more glorious future will stretch ahead of me.

During my years in the Crowborough and Brighton Daughter Lodge I have been blessed with many friends. Two of these companions were on the platform at that first service Sheila and I attended. They were Jean Le Fevre and Avis Sheppard. Jean brought into manifestation the Crowborough Daughter Lodge where she joyously worked for several years. Soon after I became a member, she relinquished her leadership and left to live in America. Since then, she has spread the message of White Eagle the length and breadth of America, Canada, Mexico and Japan. She is now spiritual Mother of the Americas and Canada. It is on her land at Montgomery in Texas that the third temple has been built.

When Jean flew off to Texas, she left the Crowborough and Brighton Daughter Lodge in charge of Avis, Reta Harrison and Arthur Patrick. Both Arthur and Reta have passed over into the light, so Avis is now our sole leader. Under her tender care the Lodge has spread its wings and we now have church services in Eastbourne and Worthing with a much increased membership. As White Eagle tells us, 'Let your light shine.' It was on the opening afternoon at Worthing that I had an indication of how pleased the White

Brotherhood were with the work Avis had done for the Lodge. I was walking along a corridor at the Friends' Meeting House, where the service was being held, when I came face to face with the spiritual body of Grace Cooke. I had never met Grace when she was alive, but I recognized her instantly by her gentle smile and shining eyes. I now know why White Eagle called her 'Bright Eyes'. As she stood in front of me, I sensed her happiness at the forthcoming ceremony, and I knew that she had come from White Eagle to say 'well done'.

It was during a retreat day at Horne Farm, in Crowborough, that I met Joan Fugeman. We were to become firm friends and are known in the Lodge as 'the terrible twins'. We have had several incarnations together, a few of which are mentioned later. We work closely together helping with the smooth running of the Lodge. I lead an animal absent-healing circle whilst Joan runs one for humans. We assist with services, teaching and meditation. I remember well the first meeting we took together. As we walked up the aisle I don't know whose knees were knocking the most, Joan's or mine. I realize that when I give a talk I am overshadowed by a white brother. I perceive exactly what I am doing and what I am saying, but the words are not mine. For a short period I take a back seat. I give him all my grateful thanks, for without his aid my work would not be possible.

I remember how much I needed this direction when I was on the platform at a Sunday service last year. I was just about to commence a prayer for humanity when the main church door burst open and into the aisle poured about fifteen very dirty-looking hippies. I welcomed the fact that they were young and hoped that they would enjoy the proceedings. I ushered them into the back seats and continued with the rest of the ceremony. It soon became obvious that they had not come to pray. There were several 'cat calls' and an air of complete unrest. When I got to the Lord's Prayer, which we sing, I realized that I would somehow have to get them to leave. There was no way we could conduct the service in peace and tranquillity. My fear was that if I spoke or acted in any way they thought offensive, they would wreck the chairs and cause complete chaos. I sent up a silent thought and opened my mouth. I welcomed them but explained that we were a healing church and needed silence in which to perform this ritual. If they wished to, they could participate, but if they were unable to be respectful would they please leave quietly. The miracle occurred; they left their seats and in an orderly fashion passed out through the door. One of them actually turned and apologized to me. I wished them well and extended an invitation to come back again if they were really interested in our teachings. The situation was saved and we were able to enjoy the rest of our afternoon, thanks to the help of the angelic kingdom and our protectors.

During my years with the Crowborough and Brighton Daughter Lodge my heart centre has grown and expanded with love for my fellow man. I have learnt the meaning of unity and realize that we are all part of the same mould and all fashioned by the same hand of God. I have gained more knowledge as a channel for healing, assisted by the beautiful method used by all Lodge helpers, which brings into play the use of colour; with the aid of healing angels we direct various shades to the different chakras of the body. We use our hands to clear congestion within the etheric field, before giving contact healing. With our inner vision we direct colours to where they are needed to ease pain and bring comfort to the patient.

The Lodge also teaches a very gentle, but at the same time very advanced, form of meditation. The students are kept safe and secure whilst being raised above the astral planes into the mental and spiritual worlds. With practice you become aware of the grand silence and communion with the collective consciousness, which is the mind of God. Symbols are recognized and interpreted, bringing answers to seemingly unsolvable questions. The complete absorption with light, which is the heart of God, becomes a reality.

Last year, Joan and I were fortunate enough to visit Jean Le Fevre in Texas. Our visit was primarily to help with the office work, but turned into one of the most memorable trips that I have ever taken. I came across some words by St Francis that Jean had published in an old Crowborough Newsletter, which will give you some idea of the compassion within Jean's soul.

The Lord give you peace, but when you proclaim peace by your words you must carry an even greater peace in your hearts.

Let no-one be provoked to anger by you, or be scandalized, but let your gentleness encourage all men to peace, goodwill and mutual love.

For our calling is to heal the wounded, to tend the maimed and to bring home those who have lost their way, for many who today seem to be the children of the Devil will yet become disciples of Christ.

On arrival at Houston, before we could start any typing duties for her, we were whisked off to an extraordinary gathering of the American Indians. Many years previously, Jean had been invited by a lady called Twylah Nitsch to visit a reservation that was the home of the Seneca Clan. Twylah was Clan Mother of the Wolf Medicine Lodge and Grandmother to many teachers, healers and medicine people. Eventually Jean was given the great honour of being initiated into the Seneca Clan and was gifted a very special feather, which she was told would link her with the Uniting of the People. This came to pass when Twylah called together all Elders to represent their people at the first Peace Elders' Council, which was held at the Cattaraugus Reservation. At this gathering Jean was initiated as an Elder, fulfilling the prophesy given to her with the feather all those years ago.

A second peace conference, called Wolfsong II, was being held in Texas, at Thunder-Horse Ranch. It was to this amazing gathering that Joan and I had been invited to assist Jean as servers. For three days we watched and listened while Elders from all over the world were initiated. They were people from every race and country, who were being honoured for their efforts to bring peace to Mother Earth. Joan and I met and communed with Aztecs, Maoris, Mexicans, Germans, Aborigines and citizens of many other cultures. Everyone had come for the same purpose, to meet and unite together for the benefit of humanity and our much abused planet. We participated in inspired meditations and sat for many hours as Elders held animated speeches and conversations. Some were, of course, in foreign languages and had to be translated. We found the Indian people to be very gentle and extremely courteous, even when Joan and I managed to sit in the wrong seats, reserved for Elders. The amenability and good humour of Thunder and her husband Horse, who owned the ranch, helped to make Wolfsong II a resounding success. Their preparations for the conference had been marred by violent thunderstorms and torrential rain, which had caused flooding just before we arrived. With the temperature in the upper nineties this had made life very uncomfortable, yet with quiet acceptance the helpers just donned wellington boots and proceeded to cover all the flooded areas with as much straw as they could carry. The rain ceased and the sun came out for all three days of the conference, at the termination of which the thunder and lightning returned; it has been said that the American Indians have control over the weather.

One of the items of ritual during the conference was the drums. The rhythmic beating of these instruments, which never stopped day or night, brought back ancient memories. I became a young brave once more, running silently through the forests with the sunlight glinting through the trees forming a ribbon of light on the path ahead. The animals were my friends, the wind and water my music and the earth my teacher.

On the second day of our visit, Joan and I beheld an artefact that I had never imagined I would see with my physical eyes. One of the newly appointed Elders, who was a dealer in precious stones, brought with her a crystal skull. How it had come into her safe keeping I do not know. It was placed on a raised table and we were all invited to look very closely at this miracle of ancient craftsmanship. Only four of these skulls have ever been excavated, and they were all found in the area where, it is believed, the ancient civilization of Atlantis once lay. One is housed in the British Museum, but is rarely on public display. It has been said that they are 'Skulls of Doom' and bring misfortune and death. The wondrous object, which we were allowed to look at, had a very magnanimous vibration. The skull had been carved out of one complete block of crystal, with the jawbone separate and hinged so that the mouth opened and closed. There were passages and chambers bored into the skull, so that a light placed behind the head would illuminate and channel the light into the eye sockets, producing the vision of flickering flames. The optics are so precise that, even with all our modern technology, we cannot build a replica of the exact proportions. As I gazed at this friendly work of art, I got the distinct impression that the skull was enjoying himself. He was delighted with all this adulation and wished to be of service to us. It is believed that they can act as transmitters, bringing back to mankind ancient knowledge and memory. In my case, this has certainly been true. Since returning to England I have been given insight into previous incarnations in the temples of Atlantis. In my next chapter I will describe two of these past lives as they were presented to me during meditation.

At the conclusion of our visit, Joan and I bade farewell to our Indian friends and returned with Jean to Montgomery. The site for a White Eagle temple in Montgomery had already been laid out and the footings put in. We were glad that we had come to help Jean, as it soon became apparent just how hard this determined woman was working for the Brotherhood of Light. As spiritual mother of the Americas and Canada she has a monumental workload. This, combined with the responsibility for the construction of the temple, would have daunted a lesser personality. Representatives from Liss come out to assist her and she has a very loyal team working with her, but in the final analysis it is Jean who makes the ultimate decisions. An example of this occurred the day before we left for England. The storms and rain had caused the newly built footings for the temple to subside. A mistake had obviously been made somewhere and the wrong materials used. After much consultation, Jean took an irrevocable decision to use an alternative scheme that could have affected the structure of the temple. I am glad to relate that The Temple of the Golden Rose has now been completed and dedicated by Joan Hodgson from the White Eagle Lodge at Liss. The light from this sacred building will shine out to all people across that vast continent. Jean, however, still gets into the office at 5.30 every morning.

Jean has also devoted her life to the care and protection of the animal kingdom. When she lived in England she worked for many organizations and was responsible for the establishment of the Kit Wilson Trust in Sussex, which continues to find homes for abandoned and cruelly treated creatures. Jean still looks after an assorted band of rescued dogs and has turned her attention to the birdlife of Texas. She has a special state licence which enables her to collect and look after injured birds of prey. It is amazing to see her handling, without gloves, these enormous raptors. They instinctively know that she is very special and will do them no harm. The centre has recently been host to a large vulture called 'Good Time Charlie'. This huge bird had become convinced that he was human and would circle the neighbourhood looking for fun and games. He turned his attention to the Christmas Tree farm just across the road, where people would picnic on a family outing. He would help them choose their trees, ride on top of their cars and eat all their food. Life was wonderful for Charlie until some children decided that they would like to play with this 'friendly birdie' and it was realized that the children and Charlie might be a danger to each other. Although Charlie was very gentle it could not be forgotten that he was a wild creature and care had to be taken. He has now left the centre and has joined an educational project which teaches Society about the beauty and wonder of wildlife.

It was with regret that Joan and I left America. We had enjoyed the hospitality and generosity of the Texan people whom we found to be warm-hearted and fun-loving.

It is said that we all teach one another once our feet become firmly planted on the path to enlightenment. I certainly found this to be the truth regarding my many friends within the Lodge. Before I close this chapter, I would just like to mention two very exceptional people.

When Eileen Turner first joined our Crowborough and Brighton Group, she was confined to a wheel-chair. Rheumatoid arthritis had taken its toll and she had lost the use of her legs. With healing and medical help, she left her chair and was able to participate in Lodge activities. Unfortunately, she also developed osteo-arthritis, which necessitated a number of operations. To date she has suffered one elbow and four hip replacements, which have caused her intense pain and great discomfort. I once visited her in hospital and found her lying in a soaking wet bed, covered from neck to toe in damp soggy plaster. White Eagle always tells us to 'Keep on, keeping on,' and Eileen is a perfect example of his teaching. She always picks herself up and carries on, disregarding the agony which often affects her every movement. Her latest hip operation appears to have been a complete success, thanks to an extremely competent Italian surgeon. I am sure that I will soon see her careering about in her car again, as she ferries members with no transport to various meetings.

A few years ago I went with Joan Fugeman on a retreat week to the temple at Liss. It was on this visit that I had the good fortune to meet Irene Hancock, or 'Radiance' as White Eagle called her. She had worked for the Lodge for fifty years, first in London and then at Liss. During the war she had been personal secretary to Geoffrey Lloyd at the Ministry of Fuel and Power and had previously been secretary to Stanley Baldwin. Radiance was our House Mother for the week, helping us with any problems that we might have and generally looking after us. It was towards the end of her life and we were the last retreat members that she was able to serve in this way. Radiance with her great wisdom did indeed know the meaning of service. It was from this glowing soul that I learnt how a true disciple should talk, live and behave. Despite the fact that she was nearly blind, Radiance had an aura of gentle love, compassion and complete acceptance. She had a wonderful sense of humour and delighted in mealtimes, when we all laughed and joked together. As Ylana Hayward wrote in her tribute to Radiance, 'She remains an example to us all of integrity, of love, of a gentle radiant spirit and the power of that gentle radiance to heal, to comfort, to illume.'

My dear companions and soul mates of the White Eagle Lodge, I would like to mention you all within these pages, but it would fill too many volumes. Suffice to just let me praise you at the end of this chapter for the wonderful work you are all doing. The bonds that we have forged in this life will stretch into eternity. I know that White Eagle will join me when I say, 'Well done, my true and faithful friends.'

UNITY WITH ALL LIFE

Before you commence your meditation, make yourself completely comfortable in your chair. Relax, close your eyes and feel as if you are being raised by unseen arms into the world of light. At the beginning of this book, we visited the cave in the hillside, which represented your heart centre. We are returning to this small cavern today. Once more see the altar with the candle flame, the spark of God within you. This time, however, you will notice how much brighter the cave appears when you step inside. The love in your heart has grown stronger and stronger and is reflected in the glorious light all around you.

For a few moments, kneel before the altar and give thanks for all your blessings. If you are in need of something for yourself, or a friend, just ask.

When you are ready, walk to the entrance and gaze at the scene before you. As you look down, observe that every country of the world is laid out before you. You will notice that all over the globe are scattered little lights. These are the heart centres of all men of goodwill who are working for peace and the healing of God's creatures on Mother Earth. As you watch, these lights appear to multiply and glow brighter. This is because you are now unified by love, from your heart to theirs, circulating this force all over the planet. In some countries the lights are many; in others, very few. Hold those sparse little lights in the ray of love that is pouring from your body. They are battling very hard to bring succour to their nation and need all the help that you can give them.

Look up into the sky and you will see that you have been joined by the four angels of the elements, earth, air, fire and water. They are waiting to take you on a journey, so that you can experience unity with Mother Earth. The angel of the air steps forward in greeting and you are aware that you are being lifted in her arms, away from the cave. There is nothing to fear; all you are sensing is calm and peace. You are now circling the earth on the currents of a gentle breeze, purifying the atmosphere and bringing healing to every tree and animal touched by this wind. You have become a part of the angel of the wind as she blows the clouds across the sky.

The clouds are causing rain to fall onto the earth and the angel of the water stands before you and is welcoming you. She enfolds you and carries you down towards the earth on the raindrops. As they enter the seas and the rivers you are within these streams and lakes. You are helping to clear the pollution and are bringing harmony to the fish and mammals of the deep.

The angel of the water fades and in her place stands the angel of the earth. As the rivers overflow and soak into the soil, you are part of all the growing seeds nestling under the ground. With the help of this angel you encourage the small plants to push up out of the land and turn their faces to the sun. The purity of your love helps to clear away the effects of chemicals and insecticides. Our planet begins to breathe once more.

The spirit of the earth releases you gently and you are held within the warmth of the angel of the fire. The rays from the sun fall upon the creatures of the world and you become absorbed in the rainbows of light, bringing health and restoration to all living things.

You have been united and become a part of all the four elements of nature. Through your meditation you have achieved union with the earth, air, fire and water as well as bringing healing to all the atoms of your own physical frame.

The picture begins to disappear slowly and you are safely back within the walls of your own cave. Pause for a short time and just enjoy the beauty of your surroundings.

When you are ready, return to your chair and, breathing a little bit deeper, enfold your body in the golden light of love and protection. Remember the words, 'As you give, so shall you receive.' The help that you have given to creation has brought you strength and you realize that you are feeling healthy and happy. Open your eyes and take up your life once more.

FOOTSTEP 6

Love from the Masters

My work on the inner planes has brought me close to three of the great Masters who watch over the evolution of mankind. They are very concerned that searchers on the path are opening up their brow and head centres, before the heart centre is fully awakened. This can cause an imbalance which holds up progression for several incarnations. It was, therefore, impressed upon me that I must write this book so that it flowed with love from my heart in a way that would be understood by all people. I hope that, with their encouragement, I have accomplished this. The Masters no longer wish to be shrouded in mystery; they want humanity to be more aware of their presence, so that they can be of help to all individuals seeking spiritual enlightenment.

Who then are the Masters? All through the long aeons of time, since man first left the heart of God as a young spark, there have been great beings of light and love who have come to teach man truth according to his need at that particular time. For instance, Osiris in Egypt, Lao Tsu in China, Krishna in India, Mohammed in Arabia, Buddha in India and Jesus in Israel. These are human beings who have trod the path before us and have experienced all the pain, suffering, joy and laughter that has been our karma on this planet. They have walked the same stony way as ourselves and have battled through until their souls and spirits have become one with the great light and energy that is God. They are 'christed' souls, our ascended elder brothers – the illumined ones. They draw close to help us to reach the same glorious inheritance, the top of the mountain. Through past ages their names have been spoken in a whisper, known only to a very few who kept and guarded the secrets of the ancient wisdom. This was necessary because of persecution and the laws of heresy. Man was not ready to receive these teachings. Now, on the threshold of the Aquarian Age, it is time for a large percentage of humanity to recognize the logic and beauty of these ancient laws. The energies pouring down on us, as we enter this new age, are forcing vast changes not only to the planet but to ourselves. We are ready for new ideas, new thinking, more tolerance and a large step forward in our religious beliefs. Now especially has come the time to recognize and embrace the existence of these illumined brethren. When a man becomes 'christed' or full of light, he has a choice. He can either evolve upwards into other realms of consciousness and higher vibrations, leaving this earth plane entirely, or he can choose to stay and help his brothers who are climbing the rungs of the ladder behind him. Many Masters, because of their great love for humanity, elected to remain within the earth's atmosphere, steadily working to bring Christ into the hearts of men. Although they no longer have any need to reincarnate, except in special circumstances, they can take on human form in order to perform certain tasks and live close to man. Mostly they inhabit the higher mental and spiritual planes coming down into the astral plane and etheric realms when necessary. They spend much of their time pouring light and love onto the earth, its countries and its inhabitants, using the heart centres of evolved mankind to perform this act. As they look down onto our world they see little points of light, which mark the existence of humans with open loving heart chakras. These lights are becoming more and more plentiful, as are larger spots around the globe, which denote established light centres, used for the healing and spiritual unfolding of mankind.

Our elder brothers work alongside the great archangels of our solar system, lovingly commanding and guiding the nature and fairy kingdom in their work. One of the questions I frequently get asked is, 'Why are Masters always men and not women?' The answer to this is that when an initiate is illumined he has one further decision to make as to which lifestream he takes form in – human or angelic. Most of the women initiates ask to belong to the angelic lifestream. They work alongside the male Masters to bring in the feminine aspect of manifestation. There are some female Masters, namely Lady Nada and Lady Mother Mary, who was the mother of Jesus.

To my readers I would say learn and digest as much about the Masters as you can and when you are ready you will feel drawn to a particular elder brother. I spent five years sitting within the aura of the Maitreya, in meditation, before I became aware of the work which he wished me to undertake — writing and teaching.

I will now try to bring you into contact with the three Masters who have become such a blessed part of my life.

The Master Jesus

There are very few people in the world, regardless of religion, who haven't heard of this great Master. All healers and helpers of humanity come under his direction. He still takes on a physical body from time to time and works very closely with the Buddha. There is a great affinity between these two adepts; they have always assisted each other in bringing the word of God to the ears of man. Jesus taught 'doing'; the Buddha taught 'being'. All students and practitioners of meditation come strongly under the influence of the Buddha. Through these two Masters the East and West will eventually unite as one; the Law of Balance or Equilibrium must be worked out. The East has thought too much about spiritual values, ignoring their material liabilities, whilst the West has pursued wealth and power with little thought of spiritual rewards. When the pendulum swings evenly between the two civilizations, bringing balance, then Jesus and the Buddha will have achieved their objectives and peace will reign on Earth.

Let us look now at the life of the Master Jesus whilst on Earth. An astrologer friend of mine has a theory that his birthday was not December, but was in fact August. This makes sense for it means that Jesus came under the sign of Leo, a child of the sun. This would have given him the strong, positive personality to which people were drawn in large numbers. We know he was a great orator and storyteller; Leos are usually on centre stage. This sign would also have given him his great compassion and love for people combined with his tremendous energy and healing ability. A Leo sense of humour would have been essential to help him through many grim situations. Israel at the time of Jesus was ruled with a rod of iron by the Romans. Life was cheap and, for the Jews, very, very hard. To stand and preach love for your fellow-man, be he Roman or gentile, must have taken a personality of tremendous wit and vibrancy. I never see Jesus as meek; he wouldn't have survived the market-place. I would say to all students of this Master, 'Go back to the new testament and read it again. Get to know this man; look deeper into his teachings and parables, which were veiled and full of inner meanings.' Two excellent books are *The Living Word of St John* by White Eagle and *The Aquarian Gospel of Jesus the Christ* by Levi.

Jesus' purpose on Earth was to be a channel for the christ spirit, which is the light or son of God. This great spirit, Christ, had never reincarnated on Earth, so had no instrument or body in which to function. Jesus was chosen as the Master who would use his physical vehicle as a channel for this great light. Over many, many incarnations Jesus perfected his earthly body to withstand the overpowering force of the christ spirit that would enter his body before the start of his teaching work throughout Israel. This, of course, happened at his baptism in the river Jordan by his cousin John. The dove descended above the head of Jesus and his mission on Earth, for the Christ, had commenced. The Easter festival is the culmination of all his hard work for the future of mankind on this planet. He knew what lay ahead of him and welcomed it. His sole aim at the end of his life was to anchor and ground the Christ light into the earth itself. Before the coming of Jesus, very few souls were advanced enough to take the tests and trials leading up to illumination. His death opened up the gates and portals of initiation to all men. At this point in history mankind had reached the end of his journey down into dense matter and with the death of Jesus could start treading the path back to the Godhead. Up to this time humanity had learnt to become individuals; now was the time for them to start the trials and lessons that would one day bring about the equality and union of all people. When Jesus' blood flowed down the cross and soaked into the soil, the Christ light was earthed on this planet and the upward arc of evolution had begun. The bible tells us that darkness covered the land, but what really occurred was that the descending light was so bright that it blinded all who looked at it and for a short time it appeared as black as night. Jesus, hanging on the cross, gave a deep sigh of triumph and with his last breath uttered the words 'It is done'. His service to this world was complete. He truly was the saviour and through his love and sacrifice our destinies are assured. All men now have the right to attain their full potential as Sons of God.

Jesus said, 'I am with you even to the end of the Earth,' as indeed he still is and will be when this planet no longer has a need to physically shine in the heavens. As I mentioned earlier in this chapter, the Masters work closely with the great archangels of our solar system, particularly the seven great angels before the throne of God. These magnificent beings work at the head of the seven great rays of manifestation, pouring the essence of these rays, each one of which has different properties, onto the earth and the inhabitants of this realm. The Master Jesus works at the head of the sixth ray, which is the ray of devotion and enfolds all the religions of our world. In our own Western churches he is always present when the Eucharist is celebrated, with the angels of light of that particular church. The same is true at any spiritual festival within any religion. As a Master he can appear in hundreds of different places at once and is always in attendance at healing services or, when asked, with individual healers. He works with the healing archangel Raphael, who can be seen projecting the beams of light from a golden goblet held against her heart centre. The colours glowing from this archangel are seen as different shades of green for healing the earth and varied hues of blue for mankind.

I have been fortunate and blessed to have seen this elder brother many times. He always appears surrounded by a golden aura with eyes of love and compassion. He has a wonderful smile full of joy and good humour. He always laughs when I go to him with the words, 'Please help me, I'm making a real mess of this.' He is human and very approachable. To any reader who wishes to make this Master a friend, I would say, as always, that the only requirement is love. Sit quietly in meditation and imagine that this brother is standing in front of you. Communicate with him through your heart and imagination will soon become reality.

The Master Ragoczy

My first introduction to this Master came many years ago before I joined the White Eagle Lodge. I was having problems and went to consult a friend of mine called Rita Keating, who is also a very good medium. She gave me quite a bit of general help and then she suddenly said, 'I see a knight in shining armour sitting on a white horse. He is totally immersed in light and is carrying a silver sword. This knight will mean nothing to you now, but he will come into your life in a few years' time when you are ready.' I thought this was quite amusing; I really wasn't into gallant cavaliers on white chargers. I forgot about this message until I joined the Brighton branch of the White Eagle Lodge. After being in this group for a little while I began to see, in meditation, a white knight astride a white horse holding a silver sword. Rita's words came back to me and I longed to know who this man was. I found out very quickly. The information was given to me when I was on retreat at the White Eagle temple at New Lands. Joan Hodgson was taking us in meditation when I had my usual vision of the white knight. Afterwards I mentioned this to Joan, who explained to me that I had perfectly described to her the Master 'R', as he is known in the Lodge, who is the elder brother who watches over all the activities of that light centre.

Over the years I found out more and more about this Master who, like Jesus, had reincarnated many times on this earth. Through his experiences, he also was able to understand and sympathize with our everyday problems. He had lived on our plane of existence as Merlin, St Alban, Roger Bacon the monk scientist, Christian Rosenkreus and the Comte de St Germain, naming just a few of these historical figures. He was also Francis Bacon, in the time of Elizabeth I. As I had always been interested in this gentleman, I read and studied what history had to say about this very learned figure. He was the illegitimate son of Elizabeth I and Robert Dudley, Earl of Leicester. It is said that he was born four months after a secret marriage between Elizabeth and Robert Dudley, a union which Elizabeth refused to acknowledge, wishing to retain her title of 'Virgin Queen'. He was brought up by friends of the queen, Sir Nicholas and Lady Anne Bacon. All his life, the queen dangled before him the prize carrot that one day she might recognize him in public and proclaim him Francis I of England. He had to learn to curb his pride and experienced many humiliations. However, he never rebelled against his mother, becoming instead one of the most brilliant scholars of that era. He brought enlightenment in science and literature to the common people of Britain as well as founding secret societies and mystery schools e.g. the Freemasons and the Rosicrucians. It is said that it was he who wrote the Shakespearian plays and I believe this to be true. He wrote in secret ciphers and drew pictures full of inner meanings; anyone wishing to study his work should read the discoveries of Peter Dawkin, founder of the Francis

Bacon Research Trust. All his life Francis had terrible money problems and was persecuted and called a swindler right up until his death in 1626. His trials and tribulations would have destroyed a lesser man, but were in fact the making of a Master. It is also believed that the Master 'R' was Joseph, father of Jesus, and this would explain the close connection between these two Masters. They work together for the continent of Europe, helping to create the unity between all the countries that we are experiencing at this present time.

The Master Ragoczy is head of the seventh ray of ceremony, Ritual and Magic. He is one of the prime helpers responsible for the dawn of the golden Aquarian Age. He loves bright colours and I often see him enfolded in a cloak of vivid purple. He works very much with the mineral kingdom and it is through his influence that mankind is discovering and using the healing power and properties of crystal. He commands the respect of great angels who are ever ready to be of service to him. Chief amongst these is the Archangel Michael, who is known by the title of St Michael and All Angels, as he is Lord of the Heavenly Forces upon Earth. It is interesting to note that Michael is also known as the Wielder of the Sword of Light, which is of course the symbol of the Master Ragoczy. The Master 'R' is also known as Master of the energy of balance and as we look at the world today we can see the spiritual pendulum swinging backwards and forwards in every field of human endeavour, working out the Law of Equilibrium. As well as in Europe, the Master 'R' is working behind the scenes in that great continent of America. When I was visiting there last year, I was amazed at the strength of the 'New Age' groups spreading across the country, all helping to bring in the Aquarian teachings ready for the time when America will be the spiritual centre for the next great surge forward of mankind.

Again I am asked the same question, 'How can I get to know this great Master?' My reply is, as always, 'Send him love from your heart centre, with a longing to be of service in the coming golden age.' I often hold an amethyst or quartz crystal in my hands as this seems to set up a special link. You may not see the Master in your meditations for some time, but he will always send a representative to guide and help you. If, however, you are aware of the smell of violets, then the Master draws close; they are his favourite flowers. I always ask for his help if I am taking a service or giving a talk on the ancient wisdom. I am never disappointed and can feel his influence very strongly as soon as I start to speak. It makes me feel very humble and at the same time very conscious of my responsibilities.

The Lord Maitreya

This Lord could well be called Chairman of the Board of Ascended Masters. The word Maitreya means 'kindliness' and this very, very, evolved being is all love. His colour is pure white light and this is how I see him in my meditations, with a face so radiant that I hardly dare look upon it, so high are the vibrations. This is the Master who came to my assistance, bringing with him the Christ light, when my need was so great whilst trying to deal with the Dweller on the Threshold. The Maitreya represents the Christ light in human form and it was his essence which poured through Jesus in Israel, assisting him to bring into manifestation the Christian religion for the Piscean Age. This Lord is also the world teacher bringing knowledge to all people, influencing all learning and stimulating the latent potential in every man, creature and angel.

The Archangel Uriel is associated with the Maitreya, working as an interpreter of God's will, inspiring and giving ideas to writers and teachers. He is the bringer of wisdom tempered with love, helping humanity to reach salvation through truth and service. He is connected with all forms of art and expression.

As I mentioned earlier in this chapter, when I first became aware of this Master, I spent the following five years drawing close to him in meditation and just sitting within the outer ring of his aura. I am told that he wasn't quite sure what to do with me or what task to give me. I had a lot of boulders to clear from my path before I could be of use to him. However, just to feel a minute tremor of his vibration would bring me back from a meditation with renewed vigour, able to cope with whatever life had in store for me. Eventually I was allowed to start teaching and the ideas for this book began to form in my mind.

Although a Master will always help a disciple who is in need, if you wish to sit within his aura during meditation I would impress upon you certain stipulations. Never go to him feeling depressed, irritated or angered. Always approach with joy and love; any negativity will be picked up within his aura, ruffling the still waters of his consciousness.

These, then, are three of the illumined ones that it has been my privilege to come into contact with. There are many more, two of whom I will just touch upon, for your interest.

The Master El Moya

This elder brother works strongly to sweep away old ideas and dogmas, stimulating and inspiring countries, leaders and their people to enter the Aquarian Age with fresh approaches and new thinking. He is representative of the first ray of will and power. He works closely with the Archangel Gabriel, messenger of news and changes. It is also said that one of his incarnations was as Sir Thomas More.

The Master Kuthumi

This elder brother is very dear to me, as he was St Francis of Assisi from the end of the twelfth century to the beginning of the thirteenth century. His love for all God's creatures still exists today and wherever animal healing is being given, the figure of a monk in a shabby brown habit will often be seen. This Master will be the channel for the Christ light during the Aquarian Age. He works strongly with the second ray of love, wisdom, which will be the ray of manifestation for the golden years. He will be overseer for the mass initiations, taken by large numbers of the population towards the end of the two thousand years of peace. The Archangel Haniel, who labours closely with Kuthumi, is a pure form of love, whom it is said resides on Venus.

The prayer of St Francis sums up the consciousness of this beloved Master.

Lord

Make me an instrument of thy peace.
Where there is hatred let me sow love,
Where there is injury, pardon,
Where there is doubt, faith.
Where there is despair, hope,
Where there is darkness, light, and
Where there is sadness, joy.

O Divine Master

Grant that I may not so much
Seek to be consoled as to console,
To be understood as to understand,
To be loved as to love,
For it is in giving that we receive,
It is in pardoning that we are pardoned, and
It is in dying that we are born to eternal life.

Complete forgetfulness of self with enfolding love for one's neighbour, regardless of blemishes, is the

key that will unlock the secrets of the major initiations, on the threshold of which will stand the
Master Kuthumi, in joyous anticipation of our great
step forward on the pathway of light.

Learn and read about all the Masters and in your
meditations you may feel drawn to one particular
name. With a pure and humble heart reach out to
him and you will not be disappointed. Your life will
take on a new meaning, your heart and head centres
will start to open and you will begin to glimpse your
place within God's plan on Earth. You will feel at
one with all life, be it animal or Master. God bless
you all.

THE HALLS OF WISDOM
AND LEARNING

Once more close your eyes and relax. You are
aware of a gradual warmth enfolding your body.
Above your head is a golden sun with rays of light
and love pouring down upon you. Feel this beam
of light gently entering your heart and lifting you
upwards, up into the world of spirit.

You see in front of you a wide avenue of trees:
magnificent oaks and elms intermingle with silver
birches and other varieties never seen on the earth
plane. Behind these trees, almost hiding them from
view, you glimpse stately buildings, in front of which
are flower-gardens and green lawns. These are the
vast museums and picture galleries, which hold all
the treasures of the world in etheric form. Nothing

of culture and beauty is ever lost; it is all here for the eye to behold and wonder at. You have only to think of a painting you would like to see and you are instantly standing before it in a vast art gallery, surrounded by all the other masterpieces of that particular artist.

However, on this occasion, our meditation takes us to another part of this street. We turn off the main path and find ourselves in a large square with Grecian-style buildings on all four sides. These are the halls of wisdom. In the centre of the square is a tall fountain with water playing and splashing into a large pool. If you look into it, you will see fish swimming slowly across the surface. Look at the beautiful colours of the goldfish and the koi carp.

In front of the buildings are marble benches and you feel drawn to one particular seat. As you sit down you become aware that next to you is a white-robed figure. Around his waist is a rope made of spun gold and on his feet are golden sandals. This is an elder brother who has come to talk with you. If you have a problem, tell him about it and you will find that an answer begins to form within your mind. This brother of light wants to help you to expand your heart centre so that the love from your soul can radiate out into the world. Sit quietly beside him and feel that your heart is expanding with pure joy. Let these waves of light from your own soul flow out into our earthly world, reaching out to wherever they are needed, be it country or person. Just surround the object of your love with light and ask that healing or help be given.

After a while the long-robed figure stands up and beckons to you to follow him. He leads you into one of the buildings on your side of the square.

Once inside, you gaze upon a very large room lit by a pure white light that appears to be coming from an opening in the domed roof. All around the room are archways leading into smaller book-filled libraries. In the main room are several groups of people, sitting around circular tables listening intently to highly evolved teachers. You now have a choice; you can either join one of the groups or pass through one of the arches and study the books filling the shelves in that smaller alcove. If you choose to enter one of the libraries, think of a spiritual subject that you would like to learn more about and you will immediately find yourself inside that particular room with all the appropriate volumes to hand. Take one of the books to a small table, sit down and open it. You may not see the words very clearly but they will have made an impression on your inner mind and when needed will be of use to you. You may not see words, just symbols. These have meanings that can be reflected upon when you return from your meditation.

Soon, alas, it is time to leave these halls of wisdom. Your elder brother guides you out of the building and you find yourself once more on the seat in front of the fountain. If you wish, you may linger here for a short while to refresh yourself, before you return to your everyday life. Let the peace and tranquillity of this special level of consciousness enter and fill you. It will remain with you as you slowly return to your chair on the earth plane. Become aware, once more, of the solid floor beneath your feet and gently open your eyes. Remember that you can always meet your friend in spirit, either in your meditations, or in your sleep. Practise the exercise that he has given you to send out love from your heart into the world. This light that you send out will be returned to you in full measure. As you give, so shall you receive. Before you leave your chair, with your inner vision see yourself enfolded in a circle of protecting light.

FOOTSTEP 7

Meditation and Dream Experiences

The art of meditation can bring a number of problems to searchers on the path. I am frequently asked the same questions. 'What is the purpose of meditation?' 'How do I start to meditate?' 'What is the best method to use?'; 'Why are my thoughts all over the place?' 'How can I stop my mind from wandering?' I will try to answer these queries and bring light onto a difficult and sometimes very prolonged subject.

I am sorry to keep repeating myself, but once again the key is love. Meditation is often taught with too much emphasis on the head centres and not enough on the heart. The heart brings into play the energies needed to raise the consciousness above the astral planes, into the realms of enlightenment. The Masters and spiritual teachers will quickly respond to the flow of love, and will do all they can to help the pupil to develop into a pure channel for the forces of truth. The ultimate goal is to become at one with God, to tune into the collective consciousness, which thereby enables us to reach our higher selves. With practice, we build a bridge between our physical lives and the higher kingdoms of spirit. Meditation should be taught slowly and gently by an experienced teacher who will guide you from week to week, ensuring that you are relaxed and happy. The lessons will, over a period of time, progress from visualization to contemplation on a symbol, or a sentence of spiritual upliftment. Over many years, or lifetimes, contemplation gives way to unity with the creative stillness, which is the mind of God. You will, ultimately, reach a place of pure light where communion with the Infinite becomes a reality.

Meditation, like your spiritual path, can be likened to a journey up a mountain. The summit is your quest, but on the way you may take several detours and experience many occurrences. Gradually, meditation will become a part of your daily life, but the most important step is actually to start to do it. I know someone who was very eager to commence and spent a long while preparing a special room. She paid out a lot of money on furniture, incense, candles and pictures and then never, ever got around to using it. If you haven't a spare room that you can use, any place in the house where you feel comfortable will suffice. Sit with your spine erect and your hands lightly resting in your lap, with the palms upwards. It is a very good discipline if you can keep to the same time each day. White Eagle always tells us to work very slowly, with no sense of rush or hurry. This is good advice, as one of the pitfalls on our path is to rush the 'gates of heaven'. An experienced initiate can achieve this harmlessly, but not a neophyte beginning his training. Fifteen minutes a day is, therefore, quite sufficient if you are just beginning your training in meditation.

Eventually you will reach a point where contemplation becomes a firm, everyday event. You will find that you can quite happily meditate whilst scrubbing the floor or peeling potatoes. Until recently my husband and I ran a small business, and I have done some of my best spiritual work whilst driving up a motorway. Needless to say, I was in the passenger seat. My husband would sometimes turn to me and say, 'You're very quiet, you haven't spoken to me for about an hour.' Although meditation is very much a means of self-development, it must also be used for the benefit of all humanity. To always employ it for one's own advancement would be to take two very large steps backwards.

How, then, can we still our minds? In the early stages of tuition this is a very, very difficult task. How many of us have sat down, all peaceful and relaxed, only to find that we have just made a shopping list for tomorrow's lunch? We each have our own method of accomplishing serenity. A friend of mine once told me her very successful routine for doing this: she gave her earthly brain its own small bedroom, with a commodious bed and very restful decorations. If it became at all irksome, giving out extraneous thoughts, she would open the door to this chamber and place her lower mind on the divan. It would fall asleep, leaving her free to continue her deliberations. When she had finished, she would collect him again and everyone would be happy. Her lower mind had rested, and her higher mind had been able to meditate without interruption.

Visualization is a very good exercise for keeping our minds concentrated. In a led meditation the lower mind is occupied and is very busy forming the scene described. It has plenty to focus its attention on, and in this way becomes more controlled and able to come to terms with stillness and tranquillity.

When I am teaching meditation, I find that men have a great struggle with visualization. They often tell me at the end of the class that although they have experienced peace and a feeling of well-being, they have seen nothing. I assure them that this is no setback as their path may be through the inner sense of intuition, rather than inner vision. If they come back from a meditation feeling more positive and completely relaxed, then they have achieved a considerable amount. Students are sometimes afraid that what they are seeing is purely imagination, and nothing more. With experience comes the knowledge that imagination quickly turns into creative perception. They grasp the fact that they are building, with spiritual matter from the mental and upper planes, visual images which are real and concrete.

It is through using this ability to contact the higher levels that we are sometimes able to tap into the akashic records, which are held on upper mental planes and record previous lives. It was during meditation that I was able to recall scenes from two of my incarnations in Atlantis. The first of these encounters also involved Joan Fugeman, who is extremely interested in crystal. A relative had given her a large piece of calcite that had been washed up on the beach at Pakefield, near Lowestoft in Suffolk, and Joan was very intrigued with the vibrations coming from this lump of rock. It was an impressive chunk of stone with an unusual colour formation. The bulk of it was white calcite, which seemed to glow with a golden hue in certain lights; other areas contained patches of blue shading down to turquoise. Joan felt an affinity with this small boulder, so we decided that it would make a good subject for a meditation group. We raised our consciousness and contemplated the rock, placed on a table in the middle of our circle. Afterwards Joan related her journey back in time. She had found herself at a period of creation when the Earth had cooled and was forming a solid surface. She said that there was little colour, just drab greys and browns. She felt that she was standing on a part of the world where Iceland now resides. Beneath her feet, she instinctively knew, was her portion of calcite, waiting to be broken off and formed into the shape it is today.

My meditation took me back a mere 18,000 years to the continent known as Atlantis. I found myself in the gardens of a temple which, I was later to discover, was used for healing. The walls were of a white material with a deep blue roof supporting what looked like a dome made of solid gold. Behind the temple was a tall mountain that was volcanic, with a dish-shaped crown. The surrounding countryside was rich with pastureland and had an abundance of strangely formed trees, which were unfamiliar to me. I was dressed in a long blue cloak and was very busy collecting different varieties of herbs to be used as healing potions.

The scene changed and I found myself inside the temple, walking down a long corridor. The walls were of a deep sea-green and seemed to shimmer from some form of concealed lighting. On either side of the hall were white pedestals, on which had been placed large pieces of crystal. Each crystal appeared to glow and throw off rays of light, reflecting the many and varied colours. At the end of the walkway was an alcove, which housed other types of rock. It was here that I came upon the calcite which is now in Joan's safe keeping. A priest in white robes had joined me and I placed my hands around the shape of the stone. I found that I was gaining strength from this object, which was a transmitter of some kind. The priest explained that it was transferring energy from the earth into my hands to be used for certain types of healing. At this point I was aware of Joan at my side and I knew why the rock had been so recognizable to her.

My second visit to Atlantis happened some time later, again during a group meditation. Once more Joan was a part of my vision. This time, however, it was to a continent with a much lower vibration. Gone was the peace and beauty. In its place was conflict and pain. It was the last days of Atlantis and panic and anarchy were the order of the day. In this incarnation I was again employed in the temples, but as a mirror-reader, not a healer. I could look into a shiny surface and see reflected pictures of the future. I had previewed and told of the downfall of Atlantis many years before so the workers in the temples of light were well prepared for the ultimate destruction of their homeland. In my meditation we were escaping from the shores of Atlantis in what I can only describe as rafts; the nearest I can get to it is our modern-day catamarans. In this incarnation Joan and I were in male forms and were sharing the same craft; I sensed that Jean Le Fevre had also been with us, but had taken a different route.

We were a long way out to sea and I was looking back towards the smoking ruins of our country. The placid mountains protecting our northern boundaries had become raging monsters of flame and molten ash. The horizon was lit up with the fury of the fires and smoke. The beauty of the orange and red sky was the aftermath of the horror afflicting the people of Atlantis. Mountainous waves crashed down onto the raft, knocking me overboard; my last memory was of sinking below the surface of the sea and falling down into the depths of the ocean, which was to be my resting place.

There are several forms of meditation taught in this country, and I have enjoyed very powerful and beautiful contemplations with the Buddhists and the Arcane School. We all gravitate to the method which we find, intuitively, the most suitable. Eastern methods, however, are not always compatible with our Western bodies and minds. Eastern meditations can put too much emphasis on the raising of the sacred fire known as the kundalini. This divine energy, released when the initiate is prepared and ready, brings with it full knowledge and wisdom to the aspirant. This serpent of fire lies coiled at the base of the spine, within the etheric body, and should be treated with reverence and great care. In the etheric body, between the chakras, are positioned very fine webs that dissolve when a disciple is ready to receive the crucible of fire. Foolish meditators have from time to time managed to awaken the energy prematurely, for the purpose of using its power. If, however, the body is unwary and unaligned, the energy will force its way up the spine, shattering and splintering all the webs blocking its path. The end result can be total mental derangement with the recipient spending the rest of his life in an institution. It can also weaken the etheric body for many lifetimes. Spiritual undertakings must always be carried out slowly and prudently.

Whilst working in the Southwick Clinic, I came across a man who had been very foolhardy in this respect. His name was Jack and he had belonged to a rather incautious group who were practising various methods of meditation. This poor soul had been sitting in a bath of cold water for several hours trying to raise the kundalini. He had been partially successful, but had also achieved a complete mental breakdown and a stroke which had left him paralysed down the right-hand side of his body.

You will understand from the above that it is necessary to strive to make our body and mind as perfect a temple as possible. We should try to control our emotions and practise kindliness, compassion and a non-critical attitude. This is again where meditation can help. In our quiet moments, we can bring into play affirmations. We can hold within our hearts certain words or sentences, which express our need for that particular spiritual attribute. Here are some examples:

I am all love and forgiveness

*I am a child of God and his light
shines within me*

*I am a healing channel for the
power of love*

*I wish to be more humble and
accept the will of God.*

Ask for the help of your guardian angel, and all qualities become possible, where there is sincerity.

At some stage in our journey on the path, and when meditation becomes a familiar habit, we find that our dream patterns are slowly changing. People who dreamt in black and white realize that their visions in sleep have become colourful. We begin to remember our adventures at night more clearly, and can sometimes interpret symbols, as we do within meditation.

On falling asleep, we all travel in our astral bodies into the realms of spirit. Our experiences can last hours or seconds; within them there is no concept of time. If we could remember, every night, where we had been, or what we had done, our daytime worries would soon be solved. Unfortunately, on awakening our dreams are muddled, soon forgotten and lost to our memory. An exercise to help with better recall is to write everything down as soon as you open your eyes. With practice your memory becomes trained and you find that you are gaining more and more knowledge of your travels whilst in slumber. An initiate or an adept has total recall and is, therefore, fully aware twenty-four hours a day.

As I have explained previously, I do not astrally project, but I have guided dreams that are not confused, and I have total recollection of them when I return to my bed. Conscious astral projection, when we force ourselves out of our bodies, can be very dangerous and, even with experience, accidents can occur. I have a friend who regularly uses this method to research the lands beyond death. She has told me of an incident that happened just after she started her investigations, whereby she completely lost her physical vehicle and couldn't get back into it again. For a while she panicked and then she remembered the cross around her neck. She grasped it firmly in her hands and prayed. In a second she was back in her body once more and safely in her bed. The cross, especially when held within a circle of light, is a very old and powerful symbol of protection. It can be used at any time when danger lurks, and should always be employed at the finish of a meditation. It seals the chakras of our bodies and prevents any unwanted negative influences from entering.

My friend was extremely spiritual and fortunately knew exactly what to do, but other people have not been so lucky and a number of deaths have occurred from this practice. Forces that are not understood should never be tampered with. When we leave our forms naturally in sleep, we are safely attached by an invisible cord that draws us instantly back when we awaken, but this is not always the case with projection.

It should never be forgotten that the astral plane is a realm of illusion, where reality is seldom what it seems. I learnt this lesson one night on a walk-about when I was watching a teacher instructing several pupils. He was extremely knowledgeable and I paused to listen on the outside of the group. Suddenly the scene changed and he was standing in front of me. It was the same figure, but he was dressed in a cardinal's red robes and was discharging some very unpleasant emanations. I turned and ran, but couldn't escape from him; he was hard on my heels. Intuitively I knew how to deal with him; I sat down and went into a deep meditation, raising my consciousness above that particular level. He was unable to match these higher vibrations and I was free to continue on my way. It had been an exceedingly valuable experience.

Most of us who are helping humanity work very hard at night. We are not always aware of this, although we may sometimes be extremely tired in the morning. 'I don't feel as if I've slept at all,' we say. One of the most worthwhile tasks is that of aiding people to cross over into the light at death. This can be especially weary work if there has been a major disaster. The victims are confused, many refusing to believe that they have died. They look down at the carnage below them, still hearing the screams and noise. The rescue workers may even be trying to resuscitate their bodies, making them even more disorientated and lost. The problem is made worse by the fact that they have probably never given a single thought to the meaning of eternal life. We try to reassure them and help them to come to terms with their own divinity.

I remember the night of the Zeebrugge tragedy. I was assisting a dark-haired young woman who was wearing long black boots. She was still struggling to get them off her feet, sobbing that the water had got into them and was dragging her down. For an instant, I became a part of her memory; I was the one in the black boots and it was I who was being pulled beneath the water. I knew exactly how she was feeling and was therefore able to comfort and love her. After a while she was taken from me and led gently away to a peaceful place, where she could rest and recover from her shock. The next day I was yawning until lunch-time.

A number of years ago, I was feeling extremely strange and drained of energy. It felt as if something had adhered itself to my aura. I became alarmed and went to consult a friend of mine who was also a medium. When she had looked carefully at my spiritual bodies she was able to explain to me that my great love for animals had compelled me to undertake a special duty. The modern horror of the experimental laboratories had led to vast numbers of animals being maimed and then killed. The immense scale of this slaughter and the fearful cruelty had left the angelic kingdom unable to cope. They needed human volunteers who would let the animals attach themselves to their auras for a short time to allow them to recover and to gain their first experience of loving contact on the higher astral planes before arriving in the animal kingdom. What my friend saw were six small pathetic cats literally sunning themselves in the warmth of my love for all creatures. I was so pleased to be able to help in this way and gladly welcomed them. It is, however, very depleting to the etheric field, so I could only manage it for a short while. Without knowing it, many humans devoted to animals perform this duty as part of their contribution to the healing of the Earth.

There have been many books written about the interpretation of dreams, all of which are extremely useful. Every dream we have, however, is only applicable to each of us as an individual. My night-time travels, on a bus for instance, may not have the same analysis as yours. I once attended a lecture in which the instructor mentioned the fact that to dream about cats was very detrimental. This worried me as in sleep I am in the company of felines at least twice a week. Were all my waking problems brought on by my visions of cats? That was a theory I could not accept, so I decided to ask for an answer during meditation.

I sat down quietly and was soon taken back to a time in ancient Egypt. I found myself in a small temple with a balcony overlooking a wide river, which I assumed to be the Nile. It was a temple dedicated to Bastet, Goddess of the Cats. Cats were, of course, worshipped by the Egyptians and anyone found to have killed a cat was executed immediately. By my side were two beautiful silver tabbies with long elegant necks, who were purring as I stroked their heads. I was even given their names, which were Ziegri and Hendron. I don't know if I was a priestess or just a servant employed to look after these exquisite animals. It certainly explained my great love for them, which I have brought through into my present incarnation. Although there was no-one else in the room to answer my queries about the use of the cats, I realized that the knowledge was within myself. These creatures were the means by which the Egyptians bridged the gap between this world and the next, which is why they were so sacred and respected. The feline visitors of my dreams were continuing this service, bringing to me friends and teachers from the world of spirit. I am often aware of them leading me into places of instruction and debate where they sit by my side quite happily until it is time to leave.

Nightmares are another form of exposure to our worst dreads and horrors. They are symbolic of the terrors within our minds and are brought, in sleep, to help us to resolve them. Maybe you are being chased by a figure with a dagger who is trying to murder you. This could signify a deep fear that you are about to be hurt in some way. The dagger could denote the cutting of emotional ties, which you are having difficulties in coming to terms with. If in your nightmare you stop, and turn to face your attacker, the figure will vanish, together with your inability to accept what the future has in store for you.

Dreams also come as warnings. There are many people alive today who owe their continuing existence to a nightmare of impending doom. These are very clear visions, in which they behold rail and air crashes yet to materialize. They catch a later train or aeroplane and, as the adage predicts, they 'live to fight another day'. Warnings can also come in the form of symbols. For example:

You are in a boat being washed out to sea – don't get too carried away by what you are doing.

Waves crashing on the foreshore – your emotions are out of control and must be restrained.

A smoking fire about to ignite – don't spread gossip which may lead to destruction and leave your reputation in the ashes.

A key breaks off in a lock and you are trapped in a small room – you need to broaden your outlook and forge another key which will open your mind to wider horizons.

Dreams will also give you a pat on the back and show you the way ahead:

A beautiful rainbow with the end of it disappearing into the earth – your path ahead is clear. Awaiting you is a pot of gold, which is usually a spiritual gift that you have earned.

Children playing happily – could mean that a problem you felt to be large is really very small and will soon pass away.

A squirrel collecting nuts – you are being given a great deal of spiritual knowledge, but this must be shared and not buried.

A book lying open with a brightly coloured ribbon marking the page – you have been taught a hard lesson, but the ribbon indicates that this is now over. Make a note of what you have acquired and pass on to another page.

Use your imagination and have fun interpreting your dreams. You will know intuitively when you have solved the puzzle of your night-time visions.

Your meditations can also be translated in the same way. Enjoy your meditation periods without feeling any pressure with regard to the time you spend. Play some soft music and let your guardian angel take you into a land of colour and brightness. Your spiritual path should be a pleasure and a delight. I see some very long faces, as people try to reach their goal. God is all love and he wishes us to be happy as we venture forth. There is a very true saying, 'Laugh and the world laughs with you, weep and you weep alone.'

A RIDE ON A DOLPHIN

Before you start your meditation, play a piece of soothing music and just relax. Close your eyes and listen to the flow of the melody. With your inner vision you will find that you are standing on a sandy beach facing the sea. The tide is out, and you have a long walk to reach the water. You have no shoes on your feet, so you can feel the sand beneath your toes; it has been warmed by the sun and washed by the water so the ground beneath your feet is fresh and clean. There is a rock pool in front of you; just pause and look down into this small patch of sea. There are tiny pebbles in the bottom, with pieces of seaweed floating on the top. Put your finger in the water and gently touch a crab crawling across the floor of the pool. Look at the perfection of this creature, who is in complete harmony with his surroundings.

Now gaze up at the clear blue sky. There are a few white clouds passing across the sun and for a while there is shadow instead of light. You can see the gulls diving and dipping into the sea looking for food. The sunshine returns once more causing the small waves to shimmer and dance as they roll and lap across the foreshore. Just before you reach the edge of the water you notice that there are some large spiral shells sticking out of the sand. You see that one of them is of a radiant mother-of-pearl. Reach down and pick it up. Hold it to your ear and listen to the sounds of the ocean, deep down into the very depths of the seabed. It is as if you are being called and drawn into the embrace of the marine kingdom.

You have arrived at the shoreline and for a moment paddle and splash in the cool salt water. Let it run between your toes and swirl around your ankles. You are a child once more, on your first seaside outing. Suddenly you become aware that you are not alone. Watching you while it basks in the shallows is a wondrous dolphin. It turns, slowly heading into deeper water, and you realize that you must follow it. The dolphin is making small encouraging noises as you wade out and start to swim alongside this beautiful creature. You tenderly touch his sides, feeling the silkiness of his skin. He begins to prod you softly with his long nose, rolling over on his back, inviting you to stroke his stomach. He is enjoying himself and unexpectedly leaps out of the water and dives down again, making a perfect arc against the skyline.

This large placid mammal is now swimming round in circles and you perceive that he wants you to climb onto his back. Smiling and opening his mouth he lowers himself down in the water, allowing you to clamber safely up his flanks. You are now riding your dolphin through the waves, experiencing the ebb and flow of the sea. You have become a part of the ocean itself, unifying with the fish, the crustaceans, the weed and every form of life. You have now been joined by other dolphins, jumping and bounding with the flow of the tides. Listen to their calls, try to interpret what they are saying. The whole scene becomes an active, harmonious melody of sound.

The dolphins are heading towards a tiny island jutting out of the water. This is where you dismount and make your way through the surf onto a beach ringed with palm trees. A path leads through the foliage and up a small hill onto a green plateau. In front of you are some very ancient stones and statues, placed roughly in a ring. As you stand in the centre, it becomes clear that this is an old and sacred place. The winds of time have blown across this barren hilltop and it is only fitting that you should add your prayers to those of long ago. Sit down on the short springy grass and let love flow out from your heart to all of God's creation within the waters of the Earth. Picture the rivers, lakes and vast oceans as pure and clear. With your mind see all the pollution evaporating and leaving the surface of the planet. The world is now flawless as it was at the beginning of time.

When you are ready, take the path back down through the trees and onto the beach once more. Your friend is waiting for you, and you know that he has also been sending his thoughts out into the universe. This creature is older and wiser than man and has evolved to the same level as the angelic kingdom.

It is time to make your homeward journey. Once more, sitting astride the dolphin, glide along on the surface of the sea. Look into the clear crystal water and see the many different and varied colours of the fish. Look into the distance and see spouting whales and frolicking porpoises. All too soon you reach the familiar beach, still wet with your own footmarks. Put your arms round your friend for the last time and then turn and wave farewell to him. He will always be there, waiting in your meditations.

Although you would like to stay longer with your thoughts, you find that you are back in your room, sitting in your chair. Keep your eyes closed while you breathe a little deeper, and see yourself enclosed within a cross of light enfolded in a circle of light. You are feeling completely at peace with the world.

FOOTSTEP 8

Thoughts on Reincarnation and the Law of Cause and Effect

Whereas eastern religions incorporate the law of reincarnation and the law of cause and effect within their teachings, here in the West arguments have always raged within the Christian denominations, who refuse to believe in either concept. Many pages and books have been written covering this vast subject but, as with all spiritual laws, it is only through personal evidence that truth becomes reality. I will therefore try to explain my experiences, through which I have gained knowledge and insight into a small section of these complicated and monumental edicts.

Reincarnation is the only interpretation of continuing existence that has ever made sense to me. How can any human expect to become an image of the Christ in one short lifetime of 'three score years and ten'? Why do we have people who devote their whole lives to serving the light, like Mother Teresa, while others only glimpse a small spark of that divine glow? Why do we have geniuses like Einstein and Mozart? Could they really gather all that learning in such a limited time? Of course not. We spend many incarnations perfecting one particular facet of ourselves, like a diamond that needs much cutting, shaping and polishing. Great artists, musicians and actors etc. don't just acquire these gifts by luck. They are learnt, through life, after life, by practice and still more practice. This also applies to healers, teachers and mediums. Our time on earth is a schoolroom, where we learn our lessons through many mistakes and eventually achieve our certificates of merit. We then return to our real life in the world of spirit where we share our knowledge with a particular group to which we belong. As with all spiritual attainments we don't do it just for our own ego; it has to be distributed for the good of all. The great wheel of destiny keeps turning while we small sparks keep evolving.

At this point I would like to pay tribute to an exceptional soul by the name of Edmund Harold. This gentleman was at one time the President of the Sussex Healers and is a splendid seer, medium, lecturer, healer and 'adventurer'. He has travelled in several countries, teaching and sharing his abilities, and at the present time is living in the Blue Mountains in Australia. He has written a number of books on spiritual development and healing. When he is in this country I always try to visit him, as I have found him to be of enormous assistance. He has given me good advice and stopped me from straying too far off my allotted path.

The first time I met Edmund, he told me of a

time when I had lived in France in the sixteenth century. He said that I had worked closely with Nostradamus as a helper with the plague victims of that time. He said that I ignored the muck and the stench, but just concentrated on the sick and dying. I meditated on his theory and believe it to be true. I remember, as a child, having a dream where I was surrounded by very sick people lying on straw beds. There was much vomiting and bleeding from the nose and mouth. I wasn't bothered by this and was busy trying to make them drink some sort of liquid from a shallow cup.

I have since investigated the life of Michel de Notre Dame, also known as Nostradamus, and discovered a man of extreme moral strength and valour. When he first became involved with the plague victims, he worked in a town called Aix-en-Provence. By the time he arrived in the stricken area, a large proportion of the inhabitants were dead. It was springtime, with birds singing and sheep grazing in the fields. In the streets of the town, however, it was a different matter. The burial carts were piled high with dead victims, on their way to the outskirts of the town where mass graves had been dug. The church bells tolled all day and the air was fetid with rotting flesh and the smell of terror and death. Corpses lay in the streets and houses stood empty, looted of their contents. It was in the midst of all this hopelessness that my work began, aiding Michel with his healing ministrations.

Nostradamus knew no fear of contagion. He believed that a clean body internally and externally would combat any dis-ease. He mixed potions from freshly collected herbs and had particular success with a blend of mulched rose petals. The first sign of this virulent type of plague was a dreadful nose bleed. When held in the mouth, this concoction of roses probably acted as an antiseptic. Nostradamus worked for nine months at Aix, during which time he had considerable success and brought optimism instead of dread to the people of that stricken town. My close association with this great man was, I think, a stepping-stone on my healing path towards the light.

Closely following my talk with Edmund came a further revelation during the time that I was working in the Southwick clinic. A middle-aged man named Alex arrived one Monday evening in a sad and sorry state. He had suffered a very serious car crash six months previously in which he broke many bones and severely damaged the top of his skull, affecting his crown chakra. Alex had been unconscious for several days before awakening in hospital and undergoing operations to mend his shattered legs and ribs. It wasn't his physical body, however, that was the problem. He found that the bash to the top of his head had left him clairvoyant. He discovered that if he looked at a person he could see clearly scenes from their past and, sometimes, their future. Alex described it as looking at a picture show, with events flashing before his eyes. To a man who had given no thought to spiritual matters, it was a fearful and hard scenario to come to terms with.

Alex came to us for about six months. During that time we gave him healing and extensive counselling. Slowly he began to accept his condition without imagining that he was going mad. We helped him learn to disconnect, so that he was not continuously clairvoyant. He became mindful of the fact that he could be of service to his fellow man. I have often wondered what happened to Alex when he stopped attending our clinic.

One night he turned to me and said, 'Are you afraid of fire?' I replied that I wasn't and asked him why he had queried this. He then told me that I had been burnt at the stake, in medieval France, for being a Cathar. I had never heard this word before and, curious, I headed for the nearest library but found little information. What I did discover was that they were a religious group with a firm belief in reincarnation, who lived in France in the twelfth and thirteenth centuries. Because of their beliefs they were persecuted and hounded by the Roman Catholic Church. Eventually, in 1244, Cathars were put to death in their hundreds at a place called Montsegur. The method of execution, as for all heretics, was by burning at the stake. I had no recollection or intuitive sense of this fate befalling me, so I forgot all about it for several years.

When I joined the White Eagle Lodge, it was with interest that I learnt of a definite link between the Cathars and the founding of the Lodge. An explanation of this fact can be found in the Preface to the Lodge publication of *The Living Word of St John*. I began to uncover more material concerning the Cathars, or Albigenses, as they were also called. They were a much-loved group of people who lived and worked mainly within the shadow of the Pyrenees. The word Cathar means 'pure' and this was contained in their teachings. They practised a chaste and gentle form of Christianity, very much in line with the instructions of the early church. There was no pomp or pageantry; all ceremonies were kept simple and their tasks were performed with love and service to the people of that area. At a time in history when life was cheap, it is not surprising that they were cherished and revered in the surrounding towns and villages. They believed that killing their fellow creatures for food was unacceptable, so they adhered strictly to a vegan policy of vegetarianism. They were skilled healers, using herbs and natural remedies to bring relief to the general community. They firmly believed in reincarnation and had no fear of death.

Their popularity and unorthodox beliefs soon brought down the wrath of the Roman Catholic Church upon their heads. The full weight of the Inquisition sprang into action, culminating in a ten-month siege of Montsegur.

It was whilst reading about the last days of this fortress that I came upon some data which brought back memories of my untimely death in France long ago. In the same region as the bastion of Montsegur were numerous limestone caves, which were used by the Cathars. Not all the Cathars were burnt alive; it appears that some were rounded up and herded into one of these caves. The entrance was sealed and they were left to die a slow and lingering death. I had swift and sudden recall. I saw about twenty people, including myself, sitting in a circle in a small cavern. We were all dressed in rather dusty white robes and had our heads bowed in prayer. I could hear the voices of several men outside, who were obviously intent on the task of sealing the cave. What little light there was soon vanished, and we were left in darkness, with only the power of our own spirits and the comfort of the Consolamentum – a ritual used at death by the Albigenses. I truly believe that when this ceremony was performed it brought the angel of death quickly to their aid. As a child I had a recurring nightmare in which I had been buried alive. In my dream I awoke to find earth and stones above my head. I would beat on the obstructions with my fists, until I at last awoke in a cold sweat. Was that an ancient memory from my past, reaching out to be understood and vanquished?

Down through the centuries has come a legend regarding the treasure of Montsegur. A story is told of two men who were reputed to have escaped down the walls of the fortress on ropes. It is said that they carried away from the carnage a vast treasure belonging to the Cathars. Some say that they were the keepers of the Holy Grail. Many fruitless hours have been spent searching for this gold. Nothing has ever been found and I don't believe a physical fortune will ever be uncovered. The Cathars were not a community who would hoard material wealth, for they shared all they acquired with their brothers. The treasure was within their own hearts. It was that spark of love that flowed out through their healing and their teachings. They had found the perfect answer for happiness – unconditional love. What riches were those men carrying when they fled down the walls of that mountain citadel? I would suggest that it was writings explaining the faith of those gentle brethren.

Once we accept the validity of reincarnation, then we are free to examine the great Law of Cause and Effect, known as Karma to eastern philosophies. Karma is the result of every negative or positive act that we have performed in our lives. This law of cause and effect is precise and exact; it can be swift or it can take several lifetimes to balance the scales. Once we understand the truth of this awesome edict, then we should accept the teachings with a glad and joyous heart. How wonderful to be given the chance to repay old debts and then move on to fresh opportunities. It is very true that as we sow, so shall we reap. My mother used to have a verse hanging in her bedroom, with the words:

> When the one great Reaper comes,
> To write against your name.
> He writes not that you won, or lost,
> But how you played the game.

With knowledge comes responsibility. We can no longer duck the issue and pretend to be ignorant. We know that when we bring grief to another person, retribution is not very far behind. We realize that when we spread gossip, the results will fall on our own heads. That still, small voice of conscience gets louder and more insistent. Once we take notice, the battle is won. As Jesus taught all those hundreds of years ago, we must learn to turn the other cheek.

I am reminded of an incident which happened whilst I was working in a chemist's shop. A man came in with a prescription from his doctor and as I was standing near the door, he handed it to me. I was busy so I asked him to take it up to the pharmacy counter, which was at the top of the shop. He took offence at my words and muttered to himself as he walked away. I turned to another assistant and said, 'It's a pity, but you can't please everyone.'

Unfortunately he heard me, with the result that I was treated to a torrent of abuse. He used some very strong words to express his displeasure. Normally, I would have challenged him, spitting back my own words of venom. This time, however, my inner voice urged me to practise what I preach. I stood and quietly let him vent his anger on me, without uttering a word. Still clutching his prescription, he moved up the shop mumbling, 'She's mental, she's smiling at me like an imbecile.'

The next day he came back to apologize. He was going through a period filled with problems, which he talked to me about. We became very good acquaintances, which would not have been the case had I lost my temper. Karma is like a ball; it can bounce back and forth over lifetime after lifetime, until one of the players calls a halt to hatred and vengeance. The karma of every country on earth expresses itself in the same way. Battles will be fought until it is discovered that love is mightier than the sword.

Forgiveness is an excellent antidote for karma. When Jesus said on the cross, 'Father forgive them, for they know not what they do,' he was setting a perfect example. With those words of pardon, he freed his persecutors from their karma; with love he dissolved all their evil acts. Can we do any less? Forgiveness is a part of unconditional love. The next time you feel that you have been unfairly treated and long to retaliate, turn the other cheek and ask that your tormentors might be absolved. Try very hard not to just mouth these words; really pray that their karma may be negated. Instead of feeling ill with fury and the need for retribution, your soul will shine with a new light and you will have taken a huge step forward.

Never forget to forgive yourself. When you are racked with guilt and self-blame the body responds accordingly and becomes a breeding ground for dis-ease. I was once asked if I would go and give healing to a woman who was suffering from digestive problems. It was the start of many visits to the home of a lady called Sarah. I arrived to find her disconsolate, melancholy and beside herself with remorse and anguish. Nine months before I went to see her, she had been forced to put her mother in a nursing home, where she had since died. For the previous six months, Sarah had been blaming herself all day and every day. She had stopped all form of physical contact with her husband, which added to her turmoil. The congestion in her mind had caused clogging within her digestive tract. The result was severe indigestion, pain and the eventual forming of ulcers. Over a long period during which I gave her counselling and healing, Sarah began to realize how needless was her self-inflicted pain. Instead of being unkind to her mother, she had given her a very comfortable last few months. The nursing home had been loving and considerate. Sarah could never have looked after her with the same expert gentleness. When her mother died, Sarah had been at her bedside holding her hand. Slowly she learnt forgiveness of self and the ulcers faded away, leaving her free to resume relationships with her husband and enjoy a very successful marriage.

Excessive mourning over an extended period of time can cause problems for the recently departed soul. Through the sorrow of their loved ones, they can be continually drawn back towards the physical plane. This can stop their progression and inhibit the work they are trying to carry out in the realms of light. It is very necessary, and human, that we should lament their passing, but not to the extent that we bring harm to ourselves and call a halt to their spiritual growth.

We can also bring karma down upon ourselves if we dare to judge another fellow traveller. It was Jesus, again, who said, 'Let him who is without sin cast the first stone.' How can we criticize another person for any crime when, several lives back, we probably committed the same offence? We are all at different stages, gaining varied abilities and paying off assorted debts. It is only a Master who can tell how far on the path of evolution a student has journeyed.

A splendid illustration of this is the story about a refuse collector. He reincarnated into a very poor family, where there were few material benefits, but plenty of love and laughter. He grew up, married and raised several children. He had no ambition and lived a very simple life of gentle kindliness. The trees, animals and birds in the fields near his home were all the pleasures he required. He spent his life collecting and emptying other people's muck and garbage. When he died, he was immediately taken up into the higher spheres of light. To his astonishment came the revelation that he was an adept who had just taken his last initiation, before reaching masterhood. His final test on earth had been to learn the lesson of humility.

It is very easy to become spiritually smug; to imagine oneself to be superior and far removed from one's earthly companions. A little knowledge can indeed be a dangerous thing. From time to time, I am informed by patients that they are on the last turn of the wheel; that they will no longer have any further need to reincarnate. I greet this news with much love and joyfulness, hoping fervently that it is the truth. I was giving healing to one dear soul who had just furnished me with this fact, when I had a quick flash from her previous life. She was very busy, quite happily throttling her husband's mistress.

An adept would never boast of the fact that he had reached a high level of attainment. He would probably sit quietly in the background, helping his fellow seekers to perform their allotted tasks. He would encourage them with placid words of wisdom, at the same time enfolding them in his aura of affectionate protection.

It is a spiritual law that knowledge gained should also be shared, although this too can bring with it heavy karma. I am constantly aware that what I teach must always be pure, and to the best of my ability, the truth. I hope that my desire to pass on my experiences is for the good of all and not to flatter my own ego. People listen and read, so the responsibility of not misleading them is enormous. I pray that the words I have written will be used for the spreading of light, and will not be the cause of offence or hurt to any other living person.

One of the most difficult exercises is to curb and control unwanted thoughts. We may be able to remain silent and thereby avoid hurting anybody, but to stop the flow of spiteful images is another matter. Our minds are like quicksilver and a malicious reflection has formed before we are aware of it. One way of combating this is to enfold the negative thought with golden light. This will dissolve any effects it might have to the recipient or to the immediate area.

What is not always understood is that karma can be negated. How often have I heard the words 'You can do nothing to help me. It is my karma, so I must put up with it.' The Lords of Karma represent light and love, so they are triumphant when one of their younger brothers wishes to atone for a misdeed. I firmly believe that if we are truly repentant then that error is erased and we are totally forgiven. This is the true interpretation of the Roman Catholic confessional. It does not mean, however, that we are free to commit the same indiscretion all over again.

As well as negative karma, we also store up good karma. All the positive acts that we have performed are noted, and help to carry us a further few steps on our road to enlightenment. At various points along our way we may choose to reincarnate in order to help others, with no thought for our own advancement. I believe this is often the reason why babies are born deformed or mentally retarded. It brings into play the Law of Opportunity, by which their families are given a chance to look after them and be of service. When they are sent to a special school, then the law reverts to the teachers and carers. Karmic debts can also be paid off in this way. If, for instance, you have ill-treated your wife in a previous incarnation, you may be called upon to nurse her in the next one.

We are all born into appropriate situations, bringing with us the exact tools to do the job. But we have freedom of choice as to how we use these tools. We may be given great wealth and power but choose to squander it instead of using it for the advancement of our fellow man. How often do we say, 'I wish I lived in his house,' 'I wish I had her money,' or 'I wish I was famous like him.' We forget that if we had great wealth and power our progression might be blocked because these wouldn't be the right implements needed in our present lifetime. Enjoyment and happiness come from knowing that you are heading in the right direction with your inner light shining out for all to see.

I have pondered long and hard to find the perfect word which will enable my readers to move forward on their chosen paths. The one I have been given is kindliness. The great Master said, 'Love thy neighbour as thyself,' and this is as valid now as it was then. We all enjoy the gift of kindness, so let us pass it on to our brothers and sisters, human or animal. In this way we can transmute our anger, envy, jealousy or hatred, thereby allowing us to polish up several facets of the diamond, which is our soul.

THE CYCLE OF LIFE

When I was training to become a channel for the healing energy, I was given a very beautiful poem. Instead of a led contemplation, I am including these words for you to meditate upon. Choose a verse and with your inner vision go out into the open fields, sit down and consider their meaning. They are believed to have been written by a Maori.

My Law – Tieme Ranapiri

The sun may be clouded, yet ever the sun
Will sweep on its course till the Cycle is run.
And when into chaos the system is hurled
Again shall the Builder reshape a new world.

Your path may be clouded, uncertain your goal:
Move on – for your orbit is fixed to your soul.
And though it may lead into darkness of night
The torch of the Builder shall give it new light.

You were. You will be! Know this while you are:
Your spirit has travelled both long and afar.
It came from the Source, to the Source it returns –
The Spark which was lighted eternally burns.

It slept in a jewel. It leaped in a wave.
It roamed in the forest. It rose from the grave.
It took on strange garbs for long aeons of years
And now in the soul of yourself It appears.

From body to body your spirit speeds on.
It seeks a new form when the old one has gone.
And the form that it finds is the fabric you wrought
On the loom of the Mind from the fibre of Thought.
As dew is drawn upwards, in rain to descend
Your thoughts drift away and in Destiny blend.
You cannot escape them, for petty or great,
Or evil or noble, they fashion your Fate.

Somewhere on some planet, sometime and somehow
Your life will reflect your thoughts of your Now.
My Law is unerring, no blood can atone –

The structure you built you will live in – alone.
From cycle to cycle, through time and through space
Your lives with your longings will ever keep pace
And all that you ask for, and all you desire
Must come at your bidding, as flame out of fire.

Once list' to that Voice and all tumult is done –
Your life is the Life of the Infinite One.
In the hurrying race you are conscious of pause
With love for the purpose, and love for the Cause.

You are your own Devil, you are your own God.
You fashioned the paths your footsteps have trod.
And no-one can save you from Error or Sin
Until you have hark'd to the Spirit within.

FOOTSTEP 9

The Fairy and Angelic Kingdoms

Evolving alongside man is another beautiful life-stream known as the angelic kingdom. This evolution stretches from the elves, gnomes and fairies, right up to the angels, archangels and 'the seven spirits before the Throne of God', the great planetary angels. The Indian word for angel is Deva, which expresses all the wisdom, power and love that is an accurate description of the angelic form.

For most of mankind angels are brought out once a year, dusted off and placed on top of the Christmas tree. For the other 364 days of the year they are ignored. This situation is, however, slowly changing. The nature and angelic realms only wait to serve humanity and as we progress further into the Aquarian Age they will play a large part in our future development. As we evolve upwards, so too will the devic lifestream. We are part of their experiences just as they should be a part of ours. Their level of perception is higher than man's; when the animal

157

kingdom reaches our level of understanding we shall have progressed to the angelic standard of consciousness and the angels will have moved further up the chain of evolution. We all walk side by side through this great adventure called life, linking and unifying all creation on this planet with all beings of the devic stream of light and love.

So how can we work with and meet these forms of light? It is not as difficult as it may seem. As with all spiritual undertakings, the keyword is 'love'. The nature spirits and angels do not have physical bodies. The lowest world that they can inhabit is the etheric plane, which is why man can rarely see them with his physical eyes. To see them we have to raise our level of consciousness to vibrate at the same frequency as the fairies and devas. It is through meditation that we can begin to achieve this wonderful union. During meditation we are vibrating at this higher level and with experience and much love we can learn to reach this elated state of being whilst going about our everyday lives and thus begin to glimpse these forms of colour and light with our physical eyes.

One of the first angels that I became aware of during meditation was my Guardian Angel. We all have one and this entity is with us throughout our lives, since the start of our incarnations. This being tries to help and guide us along the right paths and when we at last reach that level in our development when we can acknowledge and believe in him, a great joy is felt within the angelic realm. We then realize that we are no longer alone. We now have a friend we can turn to; someone who will listen and try to help us.

How then did we obtain this Guardian Angel? In

the early stages of our existence on this planet Earth, when our material bodies were still beginning to take form, we lived as much in the etheric world as we did in the physical. This was the time when angels walked with men. This was the original Garden of Eden before the fall from grace. Man was both male and female and it was when he ate from the apple of knowledge that he became two separate sexes and left the Garden and his memory of angels began to fade. However, he was not forgotten by one particular angelic friend. This friend agreed to act as his own particular guardian. What a sacrifice this being of light makes; to watch and wait over thousands and thousands of years for his charge to reach a certain stage of spiritual maturity, to stand behind him whilst he learns from his mistakes until such time as he also begins to glow with light. It is, however, from this nearness with his human charge that the guardian angel himself evolves and progresses.

So how then did I meet my 'friend'? I was meditating on a pure white candle, watching the flame begin to grow larger and larger, when I became aware that the candle and its glow had become a form of pure golden light. The form wrapped its wings of light, pure streams of loving energy, around me, giving me a sense of perfect peace, a feeling of great calmness. I asked the entity who he was, although I already knew the answer within my own soul. Since then we have met many times and had many conversations. I still make errors and I am sure I often sadden my friend with my thoughtlessness, but I know he is always there waiting to help if it be within his power.

An angel can only help if it is in the will of our

souls. He cannot interfere if what is happening to us is part of our karma, or a lesson that has to be worked through. He can, however, stand back and offer love and support. Once you become aware of angels, life is never quite the same again. Devas are, of course, neither male nor female but it is easier for me to write about them as him or her.

One of my greatest pleasures is to sit in meditation and watch the nature spirits and fairies at work. With practice, through meditation, you can also begin to see them in the countryside with your physical eyes. They work on the etheric bodies of trees, plants and flowers, creating and perfecting many colourful and varied forms. They work in groups and are very happy and lively, enjoying themselves like little children. They can also be very shy and if they do see a human they will frequently run and hide. They do not understand why we look so glum; life to them is all happiness and beauty. They can also be mischievous, and the tales of the revenge of the Irish pixies are quite true. We must always greet them, in our meditations, with love and respect. Each group has its own devic overseer who watches over the nature spirits' work. Each valley, garden or wood has its own particular angel who stamps his consciousness on that piece of our planet Earth. Through their own accomplishments the nature spirits progress and eventually become devas. The pollution of the planet is causing great concern within the angelic world. It is holding back their evolution because of the dreadful work which has to be done, within the etheric body of the Earth, to dissolve and clear these chemical nightmares. Man does not realize the damage he is causing to himself and to other realms of existence, by trying to play God and going against the natural forces of this Earth. The black spots of this planet stand out and confirm to the rest of the universe how much further mankind must travel before the love within his heart overcomes his ego and his urge for power.

The trees are the most advanced of the vegetable kingdom and each tree or group of saplings has its own deva. This great being envelops and towers over the tree, protecting and watching its growth under the hands of the tree elves and pixies. It is possible to learn to see these angels with your physical eyes. Find a large tree and stand back from it so that you can see the whole trunk and branches outlined against the sky. Close your eyes a little so that you are squinting or looking out through the slits of your eyes. Gaze at the top of the tree and you should begin to see a faint halo of light over the treetops. This is the beginning of the etheric form of the tree deva. The whole body of the angel takes on the colours of the tree – greens and browns and russets, with the heart centre of this being radiating with light and love all through the physical manifestation of the tree. Whenever I cuddle the trunk of a tree I always send love to the deva asking for his strength to flood into me so that we might become one with all creation. Try this if you are tired and drained of energy and you will feel a tingling running all over your body, which is the deva joining you with the life-force of the tree, blending and healing. I know a stick-maker who always asks the deva for permission before cutting a branch for his craft, thus ensuring that his sticks are living pieces of wood rather than dead firewood. I also work with wood as a craft, raising birds and other animals onto plaques. Whenever I have finished a batch I always ask that love go with them to wherever they are sold, bringing peace and harmony to that particular house. People ask me what happens when a tree is cut down. I am told that the deva returns to the higher spiritual planes to await the time when the tree again reincarnates as a young seedling. This way the tree and the deva evolve together.

This brings me to the angels of the animal kingdom. Every animal has its own group soul with its own group angel, who guides and directs that particular life-form. On death, the animal returns to the group soul until it is time to reincarnate again. All life is ever-changing and never more so than with the domestic animals who, through contact with man, are developing individual souls. Consequently many do not now return to the group souls. I shall go into more on this subject in the next chapter.

Joan Fugeman and I had a very interesting encounter with a group deva two or three years ago whilst visiting the White Eagle Temple at New Lands. Joan Hodgson and Ylana Hayward were extremely concerned about the encroachment of moles all over the beautiful lawns encircling the temple. As far as the eye could see there were lumps and bumps sticking out from the grass. A multitude of moles were enjoying the hospitality and peace of this enchanting part of the Hampshire countryside. The residents of New Lands had tried every humane way possible to shift their unwelcome guests, even playing loud 'pop' music to try to persuade them to move elsewhere. No luck; the moles were aware of the harmonious atmosphere and had no intention of departing this year, next year or ever. Joan and I asked Ylana if we could sit on the lawn and try and make contact with the mole deva. She gave her permission – anything to help in the moles' speedy removal. Joan and I meditated for about twenty minutes, both of us making contact with the deva. Afterwards when comparing our experiences, we were astonished to discover that our descriptions of the mole deva matched exactly. What we both saw was an angel of light with the head and features of a mole, with the paws and long claws blending in perfectly with the rest of the deva. We both went our separate ways and it wasn't for some time that we heard the possible result of our meditations. A man arrived at New Lands offering to remove the moles gently to another area some distance from the temple. He enticed the moles out of their burrows onto a shovel, and transported them cheerfully to their new home. The moles were content, the deva was happy and so were the residents at New Lands.

There are also specific angels who look after our much abused planet. These are the angels of the earth, air, fire and water. Their helpers, who work with them, are the salamanders, water sprites and air sylphs etc. If we wish to help to cleanse this Earth, then it is essential that we ask for the aid of these angels in our prayers and meditations. The beauty of these beings, as they work ceaselessly to shift the pollution and heal the ozone layer, is beyond description. They also pour their love down onto the inhabitants of Mother Earth regardless of the senseless destruction of this planet by mankind. Let us hope that the Aquarian Age will bring harmony and the ability of all life-forms to join together in love, peace and unity on the most beautiful of all the spheres in the Universe – Earth.

It is to the healing angels that I am constantly drawn. These light forces are always near to us waiting to be asked for their help and service. You don't have to be a healer to obtain their loving ministrations. Anyone with a sick child or a close friend who is in need has only to shut their eyes and summon a healing angel and that being of light will be with them. You will then be aware of a feeling of warmth and comfort; the loneliness is less and you know you are no longer on your own. Never forget to give them your thanks and your blessing; it was always their destiny to share in man's joys and sorrows.

When humanity first began to evolve dense bodies on this planet, great forces of light called 'Lords of the Flame' came to our aid to help us to develop a brain so that we could think and reason, and thereby become individualized. When their work was complete they returned whence they came, some say from the Sun, others say from Venus.

Angels are very much builders of form, whether they are working on the trees, flowers or man's etheric body. It is interesting to note that in our healing circles within the White Eagle Lodge, we invoke the help of the 'Sons of the Flame'.

Healing angels are always present in institutions where there is great sickness, for example doctors' surgeries, hospitals, hospices and healing sanctuaries. I have always seen them with my etheric vision and over the years have glimpsed them many times with my physical eyes. They are pure light centres shedding the predominant colours of blue for healing and pink for love, with rays of light streaming behind them just like wings. I am aware of faces of great strength and beauty but it is to their heart centres that I am always drawn. These are vortices that are radiating and sending forth energies of pure love and healing onto and enfolding the sick patients.

It may seem sometimes that the patient has not responded to the angels' touch, but healing works on many different levels, not just the physical. This is never more so than at death. It is part of a healer's responsibility to help to bring to a dying soul that magnificent entity known as the 'Angel of Death'. In this way the terminally ill person makes the transition into the world of spirit without any difficulty. I have seen the Angel of Death at the bedside of dying friends on two occasions, the second of which was in Southwick at the home of two special people, Tony and Jean Robbings. This couple loved and worked very hard for the animal kingdom; they were devoted to all God's creatures. When I first knew them they had seven cats and were feeding countless numbers of birds, horses and foxes. It was a great shock to everyone when Tony suddenly developed an illness in his chest and was diagnosed as having cancer of the lungs. He went into hospital where he survived major lung surgery and was then sent home to recover. I visited him two or three times a week to give him healing. He was always cheerful and bright and all through his illness I never once heard him complain, even though he was often in great discomfort. When I first ministered to him he was very sceptical, not really believing I could help but too polite to refuse the healing that his wife Jean had asked me to give to him. However, soon he began to feel the benefit of my frequent calls; it was taking away any pain and keeping him alert and mobile. Unfortunately, he slowly began to lose weight and grow weaker and after several months Jean and I knew that it would not be long before Tony passed over into the light. It was the day before he died that I last visited him. I worked on his very thin body for about twenty minutes and was about to finish when he said in a whisper that he was enjoying it so much that he would like me to continue, which I gladly did. After a few moments I became aware of a change of vibration within the room. I looked towards the corner near Tony's bed and saw a shape of pure white light forming. It became so bright that I knew that I mustn't look directly at it or I would be blinded. Within my mind I heard the words, 'I am waiting to take him, when you have finished.' Tony died the very next day whilst I was away giving a talk at Lewes, but I am sure that he couldn't have been in better hands. A few months later I saw him in meditation, on the astral plane, surrounded by his beloved animals who had gone before him. He was smiling and happy – the same beautiful soul that I had known on our dense physical Earth.

After these experiences, how could I ever be frightened of the moment of passing. The Angel of Death is often portrayed as a horrible black image, but the entity I saw was one of pure love and understanding. To be held in his arms would be to experience the moment of death as touching the lips of God. No more pain, no more fear, just pure ecstasy and rebirth into our rightful home in the realms of light.

The other angels I am sometimes able to see are those connected with worship and ceremony.

Wherever prayer is offered up sincerely to the great spirit whom we call God, angels and archangels form. They are always present at the sharing of the sacrament, at a wedding or a christening. They work to raise the vibrations of the church or temple regardless of creed or colour. We are all worshipping the same being, equal in the eyes of God. I see the ceremonial angels in colours of gold and purple, with their heart centres open, focusing love and compassion onto the congregation. They are aware of all the prayers being offered and use the energy from these devotions to direct help and healing to wherever it is needed. No thought is ever wasted.

I am often asked why the little people dress in human clothes. The reason is that the nature spirits look up to humanity and love to copy them; there is no better way to do this than to put on trousers, coats and shoes. I heard, at a seminar, a delightful story of elves and pixies at a church service. In the particular parish where this story unfolds, the congregation were fortunate enough to have a vicar who was extremely dedicated to the word of God. The church was always full on Sundays and because of this man's spirituality there were large numbers of angels in attendance. So too were the little folk. The vicar, however, had a very jerky walk and an unfortunate habit of clearing his throat and bouncing his spectacles up and down on his nose. A medium sitting in the front row could hardly contain her laughter when she saw the priest coming up the aisle followed by a procession of gnomes etc. dressed like the man of God, walking with unsteady legs, coughing and raising little glasses up and down on their noses.

Needless to say the angels love happiness and joy as long as the joke is not of an unkind or sadistic nature.

I am certain that at various times, for the progression of mankind, the same ideas take root with several people in different countries scattered all round the globe. After working with angels over a number of years, asking for their help with a variety of projects from guarding my home to looking after my cat, I came across a book by a lady called Terry Lynn Taylor entitled *Messengers of Light*, published in America in 1989. In it the author explains how angels can help us in our daily lives. She tells about the angels of money, angels of work and angels who will help with every experience we encounter from day to day. Each chapter is practical and it is obvious that Terry is a well-adjusted and very sensible human being.

Just recently my husband, who does all his own repairs, had been having a lot of trouble with his van, which is very necessary for our work and if broken-down affects our ability to earn a living. He really was at the end of his patience. He had spent the previous two hours trying to fit a spare part in the engine. It would not line up properly; he was working at an awkward angle and his arms and hands were getting very painful. I went indoors, sat down quietly and asked the angel who guards our vehicle when it is being driven if he would please send someone to help Peter out of his predicament. My husband came in about five minutes later, grinning from ear to ear. 'You'll not believe it,' he said, 'it just suddenly dropped into place.' I said a very heartfelt thank you to my invisible friend.

I have learned, however, that with some angels

you have to be very specific. You must tell them exactly what you have in mind, or you may get some strange results. Some months ago, I was running two weekend healing workshops. One workshop was fully booked, whilst the other one was only half full. I was teaching at the half empty one first and on the evening before I was due to start I received a telephone call to say that because of an accident, two of my pupils could not attend. After giving them my sympathy, I realized that I needed at least one other person for my course. So I sat down and asked the angels, who were gathering for the weekend, to find me one more interested party for my workshop. Half an hour later the phone rang and a very nice female voice on the other end was enquiring if I had any spaces on my weekend course. I happily said, 'Yes, I shall be delighted to see you tomorrow,' when the voice replied, 'Oh, I can't come this weekend. I was enquiring for the following Saturday and Sunday.' I had made the mistake of not telling the angels the dates of the weekend for which I needed an extra person.

I have already mentioned the great archangels who work closely with the Masters to bring benefit to humanity and our planet Earth. However, one great angel that we must all learn to assist is the Archangel of Peace. He spreads his wings of healing energy all across the areas of conflict on our globe, enfolding countries and humans at war with themselves and each other. To assist the Archangel of Peace, link with the Christ light from this Archangel and hold this pure white beam over all lands that are in torment. Pray that peace may come to our planet and that leaders and heads of state will be filled with wisdom and humility. If we could use the media to spread this message of hope and peace all round the planet, how much quicker would the golden age of understanding dawn and how much quicker would mankind become children of light themselves.

In conclusion, start to welcome the angelic kingdom into your life; it is not at all difficult. Welcome the nature spirits into your garden and watch the difference it will make to your produce. Open the door of your home to the angels and bring harmony into your everyday living. When you enter a friend's house greet the angel of that hearth and bless all who reside within the walls. Let tenderness and kindness rule your thinking; let love and peace be your goal, so that the vibrations of the angels will surely hasten the time when all humanity will unite in friendship and all the dark patches on our earth will be replaced with light.

A WALK IN THE COUNTRYSIDE

Within your mind, through meditation, you are going to take a walk in the country. You will see and enjoy the beauty of your surroundings far more strongly than you have ever done with your physical senses. Just relax and close your eyes, feeling yourself being lifted very, very slowly into the world of spirit. You are not alone, your guardian angel is behind you wrapping you in her wings of love and protection. With your inner vision you will find that you are looking down on to a valley. On all sides are towering mountains, the tops of which are capped with snow. You will begin to see a bright light shining between the peaks of the mountains, hovering over the valley itself. As you look closer, you will see that this shimmering light is an angel. The colours pouring down onto the countryside are the shades of nature itself, with many different hues of brown and green and hints of blue, red and yellow. You may not be able to see clearly the face of the angel, but look at the heart centre. It is one large vortex of light and colour, a cavern of love and regeneration for this small vale, this tiny part of God's kingdom on earth.

You can now feel yourself being gently lowered, moving downwards into the valley itself, gazing at the tops of the trees that make up part of a large wood. If you look closely you will see the outline of a tree deva expanding its aura as if to welcome you into its world. You have, at last, come to rest at the bottom of a mighty oak. Reach your arms, as far as you can, around the trunk and place your cheek against the bark. Feel the heartbeat of the tree and let the life-force flow through you. Thank the tree deva for its strength and energy and leave it with the gift of your love and unity.

You will see in front of you a tiny path leading through the woods. As you walk along, notice the spring flowers on either side of you. Stop and look at the wonderful detail of shape and colour contained in a single daffodil bloom. Bend over and study a violet and, without picking it, hold it between your hands and smell its fragrance. Now listen to the song of the birds and feel a soft breeze on your face. It's wonderful to be alive on such a day. Never mind about any of your troubles; forget them. Just enjoy this moment. Now you are familiar with the pathway, let your eyes wander from side to side. You are being studied very carefully by the nature spirits. Do you see them hiding behind the bushes and the high grasses? They have decided that you are a friend and are coming out into the sunshine so that you can see them. The elves and the pixies are dressed very much like a human man, with trousers and jackets in shades of brown and green. They have little boots on their feet and caps on their heads. Some of them are busy working on the trees and undergrowth, stroking the etheric body of the plants into suitable shapes, making sure that there is no break in the aura of the vegetation. There are tiny fairies dressed in the colours of the flowers that they are attending, all working happily for the beauty of nature. A walk in the garden, on the earth plane, will never be quite the same again.

You now find that you have come to a clearing in the woods. You see that you have been joined by many small woodland animals. On the other side of the glade is a brown fox with a magnificent brush. You notice rabbits and field mice together with squirrels, and on the branch of a tree a tawny owl. The nature spirits have arrived in the clearing and all seem to be waiting for something to happen. Suddenly a shaft of light strikes down into the glade, illuminating the whole area. A form takes shape and you realize that it is the angel you saw on your journey to the woods, who is the keeper of the valley. She is the overseer in charge of the work which is being done by the 'little people' of the vale. She has come to bless the whole of the area under her control and you realize that she wishes you to join her in this task.

As the light from the angel pours down, feel it entering and flooding your heart with love. Let this love flow out from your body, encompassing and surrounding the whole valley, entering every tree, shrub and flower. As this blessing touches all the living objects in this valley, it also blesses and strengthens you. Just bathe in the glory of the light, which is God.

All too soon the picture begins to fade and you are looking once more at the treetops as you pass between the mountains on your journey back to the physical world. You are surprised to feel the familiar chair beneath you and your feet firmly back on the floor. It has been a wonderful experience and one that you can use again for the benefit of your own garden, allotment or just a stretch of land that is in need of help. Breathe a little bit deeper to make sure that you have returned fully from your meditation, encircle your body with light and love and take up your earthly life once more with renewed vigour and determination.

FOOTSTEP 10

The Mineral, Vegetable and Animal Kingdoms

During the period when I was collecting together material for this chapter, I experienced a deep and very relevant meditation. I was taken back in history to a period about 3,000 years ago. This was a time of ancient and sophisticated civilizations. Solomon was building his temple, and the Egyptian and Chinese dynasties were flourishing. Despite these facts, the earth was sparsely populated and the other three realms of nature were prominent.

In my vision I was looking down on to the Earth from a position in space where I could see a large proportion of our incredible planet. The great Law of Equilibrium, or Balance, held sway within the three lower kingdoms of nature. Everything was in perfect harmony, with each realm complementing and enhancing the other two. Man had not yet started to meddle and interfere with the scheme of God. Humanity, in those days, considered himself inferior and not superior to his creator. As I gazed at the scene before me, I was aware that I was now observing the earth from several miles beneath the surface. I was being shown the various rock strata, with each layer shaded from light brown and pale green to deeper and darker colours. I was suddenly regarding the inside of a subterranean cavern with stalactites and stalagmites. The walls appeared to be studded with clear and amethyst quartz crystals. There was a river of water rushing through this underground cave, which my eyes followed, tracing its path back to the earth's face. My sight was then drawn to vast forests, stretching hundreds of miles in all directions. Everywhere I looked it was pure and unspoilt; free of pollution and acid rain. There were no dark spots on this globe marking areas unable to sustain life. I watched wild herds of animals running free, through endless stretches of grassland. Lions and elephants with their young were parading under shady trees, never knowing the fear of man's intrusion. The word culling had yet to be formulated. In this world, nature had her own ways of checking over-population. The angelic kingdom and the realms of nature harmonized together, in perfect rhythm with the Law of Balance. I had been shown a paradise, which had been put under man's protection, to be used for our spiritual development. We had been chosen as nature's caretakers with a sacred duty to perform. We may well hang our heads in shame when we look at the total disregard that has been shown towards this dominion. I do feel, however, that mankind is slowly becoming mindful of what he has done. Hopefully, with love, it will not be too late to redress the balance.

I have already mentioned that on the upward

spiral of attainment, man will one day reach the consciousness of the angels. The animals will move to the level of humanity, the vegetable kingdom to the animal stage of perception and the mineral to the vegetable grade. Nothing in life, at any time, ever stands still. The animals are moving very fast up the chain of progression and when they reach our standard, they will have evolved very much further. The same will apply to us at the angelic level. Whereas, however, the three lower kingdoms will advance with relative ease, large numbers of humanity will fall by the wayside. These stragglers will have to wait for many, many years until the opportunity again presents itself, allowing them to continue with their spiritual growth. Realization of the importance attached to the opening of the heart centre could well halt the encroachment of this prophecy.

Let us never forget that we are all part of that loving energy which we call God. Every form of life is made up of the same atomic structure: energy that is in perpetual motion, always changing, ever moving upwards. We are all united in this great stream of activity. There is no separation between mankind and all living forms of life.

We will look, therefore, at the role humanity plays in the evolution of the other three kingdoms of nature who inhabit Mother Earth.

The Mineral Kingdom

The mineral realm is the most dense of all the

kingdoms of nature. It has a physical body and the commencement of a simple etheric body. For the minerals to progress, they need the co-operation of man. They need to be forged, shaped and moulded so that they can be of service to their brothers. Man has been achieving this since he discovered flint and lit his first fire. Our ancestors were ingenious craftsmen who worked copper, silver, gold and gemstones into decorative creations of exquisite beauty. This does not, however, give humanity the right to pillage the earth of all its natural resources, leaving our planet drained and structurally damaged.

The initiates of the mineral kingdom are the gemstones and crystals. They were helped, in their advancement, by the Atlanteans and then the Egyptian and Mayan civilizations. In the temples of Atlantis gems and crystals were used for healing, meditation and the transference of energy. It is said that they were even utilized for supplying lighting and power. It is also hinted that the Essene brotherhood in Israel were keepers of much of this progressive knowledge. In the dark period of the Middle Ages, most of this information was lost, with only a glimmer kept alive by the mystics of that time. It was then brought through by secret societies like the Rosicrucians and the early Masons. The time has once more arrived when there is a realization that these inanimate objects contain healing and regenerative properties. It is again being discovered that each gemstone has different remedial abilities, which interact with man. For example, a Rose Quartz crystal can be used as an aid for awakening the heart centre. It will restore emotional balance, give courage and transmute negativity. Amethyst is a wonderful healing stone and can be held by the patient to purify and give energy to the endocrine and immune systems. It is also a powerful crystal for meditation and channelling. It helps to open the third eye and the crown chakra, so when used in combination with Rose Quartz it becomes a perfect tool for spiritual development. Each figure of the zodiac has a gemstone which is compatible with that particular sign. In other words, the different rays or energies that vibrate through that specific sign also pulsate within that jewel.

I have always found that crystals which have been given to me as gifts have a special significance. They have been chosen with thought and when I hold them in my hands they immediately invoke a feeling of warmth and love. When picking a stone for myself, I hold my hands just above each item on display. I may experience a sense of heat or a definite drawing towards one precise object. Last year, I was in the Natural History Museum in London, looking round their wonderful 'Rock Shop'. On a shelf I beheld a very soft salmon-pink stone. I could see very clearly the outline of a face on its surface, and knew that it was calling out to me, almost commanding me to purchase it. It was on show in a clear plastic box, on which was written 'Stilbite, Poona, India'. I took my purchase home and for a long while purposely didn't touch it. I intuitively felt that it was waiting to help me with a special undertaking. When I became involved with the writing of this book, I knew that the moment had come for me to hold my piece of rock. It was my symbol of knowledge, which I could gently grasp in my hands when the flow of inspiration became a mere trickle. I call it my 'Master' stone, for it opens up passageways onto the higher mental plane. The angel of that rock was waiting with the key which would unlock my door to greater perception and discernment.

The mineral kingdom also sacrifices itself for the vegetable realm. All trees, plants and flowers gain their sustenance from the earth. They draw into their roots the trace elements and properties needed for their growth. Through this arrangement they flourish and bloom, giving both pleasure and succour to the animals and humans who live alongside them.

Through contact with mankind, stone and mineral objects can collect a degree of negativity and karma. If used for destructive activities this will reveal itself in the aura surrounding the article. This is what happens when we forge the metals of the earth into instruments of death. A gun or cannon is fired resulting in death and bloodshed, the horror of which remains attached to the offending weapon.

Many years ago, I was asked by an acquaintance if I would visit her home to see if I could sense any unusual vibrations. Her whole family were being afflicted by a series of disasters and she felt that something was wrong within the house itself. Where she had once felt happy and glad to enter her front door, now she didn't want to return there at the end of her working day. I duly went along at the appointed time, wearing on a necklace my favourite crystal for protection. On entering, I asked that the Christ light go before me to illumine any dark recesses. I wandered through the rooms and on going into the living-room I knew that I had found what I was looking for. A strong force of negativity was coming from a glass cabinet in one corner. Inside were arrayed various small objects, which looked like a collection of metal artefacts. When questioned, the lady said that they had all been dug up by her husband, whose hobby was metal detecting. I knew all about this, as Peter and I had enjoyed this activity, spending many happy hours on footpaths and the beach with a machine designed to pick up the presence of metal. I had found it fascinating to unearth coins and other items from ancient history.

I continued my search of the cabinet and soon discovered what looked like an old dagger. It was difficult to distinguish its shape as it was very battered and worn. However, when I held it in my hand it sent shivers down my spine and I got a strong impression that it had been used as a sacrificial instrument. I suggested that she ask her husband to dispose of this lump of iron by taking it back to the open countryside and laying it to rest once more, deep beneath the soil. This they did and the atmosphere within their home returned to normal, and the household was once more bright and sunny. I would add that situations like this are very rare, but strong influences can reach up through the centuries gaining entrance to our modern world.

The Vegetable Kingdom

The vegetable kingdom has progressed slightly further than the mineral kingdom. It has a physical body, a strong etheric and the first stages of an astral body. The astral plane is the area of emotions and plants are capable of responding to warmth and affection. It is well documented that if houseplants are given love and talked to, they will flourish more than those left to their own devices. I have a number of houseplants growing in my lounge — which also happens to be the room where most of my healing work is carried out — and they obviously thrive on my loving ministrations. They trail across the floor and up the wall before leaning over my husband's chair to tickle his neck. I dislike chopping them back, as they tend to sulk and refuse to flourish.

Man, once more, helps with the evolution of the vegetable kingdom by nurturing it and using its resources for food. Vegetables, again, sacrifice themselves for the benefit of humanity. We grow and cook them to sustain life; without this nourishment we would die. It has been realized, however, that eaten raw they are far more wholesome and health-giving as the vitamins and trace elements remain unspoilt, which is not the case when they are cooked. The Essenes, with whom Jesus spent some of his youth, were vegetarians. It is said that they ate only the fruits and berries of the earth that grew above the ground; they would not pull anything from the soil by its roots. In this way they were able to work very closely with the angelic kingdom. Very few of us at the present time inhabit bodies that have evolved sufficiently to stand up to this rigid diet. This situation, however, will change within the next few hundred years. Already growing children are refusing to eat meat, much to the consternation of their parents. If all men turned to vegetarianism, there would be enough land to feed all the world. Vast acres would not be used as pasture for animals destined for the slaughterhouses.

When cultivating the vegetable kingdom, it was never the intention that man should develop pesticides and chemical fertilizers, which have caused immeasurable damage and anguish to this realm. However, I am pleased to say that this situation is rapidly altering. Gardeners and farmers are becoming aware of the word 'organic'. I notice that the farming and gardening programmes on television contain many references to organic methods and natural compost heaps. Farmers are beginning to put back the hedgerows bordering their fields. They are recognizing the important part the worms, birds and wildlife play in the normal control of pests and diseases, and that hedgerows protect crops from wind and other elemental damage.

The initiates of the vegetable kingdom are, of course, the trees. They are quite content to surrender themselves for the evolution of mankind. Beautiful objects and houses have always been made from wood, and paper was invented and produced so that we could keep a record of our history and achievements. But the mass destruction of the woodlands and rain forests, so that man can manufacture more and more useless consumer goods for wealth and riches, has got to stop. The whole balance of the Earth has been upset, and the results to our climatic conditions will be catastrophic. We are damaging the lungs of our planet, a condition that will have to be reversed very, very shortly. In a strange way, however, the environmental crisis has allowed mankind to stop and ponder his inheritance. There are young men and women coming into incarnation who are striving valiantly to solve the environmental problems. Never forget that what we sow in this life we may well have to reap in our next dip into matter.

Another benefit which we derive from the vegetable kingdom is the use of herbs and plants for healing. Former civilizations recognized that herbs and plants contain remedial properties for the relief of almost any ailment. It is said that for every disease known to man, God planted a natural cure somewhere on the Earth.

As with all remedies, herbs and plants must be used with care as even natural products can have side-effects. My husband was suffering from a mild form of arthritis in his hands, so I went to my local health store in search of a treatment. I read all the labels on the jars and picked the one I thought would be the most suitable for Peter. He took the prescribed dose of two tablets and within ten minutes had turned a wonderful shade of pink. His hands were puce, his legs were puce and so was his face. He also felt extremely hot and uncomfortable for about two hours, until the symptoms wore off. As we were dealing with members of the public on that particular day, it was very embarrassing for him. It really looked as if he was permanently blushing or had spent too much time in the sun. Obviously, he had had an adverse reaction to the treatment and immediately discontinued the course.

One of the safest and gentlest of curatives are the Bach Flower remedies that treat the cause of the disease, rather than the symptoms. For example, Cherry Plum for desperation and fear of insanity, Gentian for doubt and lack of faith, or Wild Rose for apathy. The thirty-eight remedies were discovered by Dr Bach through a combination of intuition and suffering. The energy within the flower is extracted and used to treat patients. I always carry a vial of Dr Bach's Rescue Remedy in my handbag in case it is needed in an emergency. A few spots of Rescue Remedy on the tongue are extremely useful for treating shock following an accident or bad news. Bach's Rescue Remedy is also helpful for nervousness due to a job interview or an examination of any kind. There is even an ointment version which is a wonderful healing balm for burns or lacerations.

Before completing this section on the vegetable kingdom, I must just mention another realm which lies between the vegetation and the animals. This is the viral kingdom, invisible to the naked eye and unheard of before the twentieth century. This dominion is also in revolt against humanity. We have again intruded and tampered with something we know little about. If used sensibly antibiotics are a very beneficial tool, but doctors have been issuing them like children's sweets. This has resulted in the weakening of our immune systems to such an extent that we can no longer cope with the germs that are attacking us. New strains like Aids and ME are taking their toll and could well be the revenge of this particular realm.

The Animal Kingdom

In line with the previous two kingdoms, animals have strong physical and etheric bodies and are building fairly efficient astral vehicles. They are also starting to develop their mental forms. Domestic animals like dogs and cats are following man's example and are beginning to reason. Anyone who challenges this statement cannot have had the great pleasure of sharing their home with a much-loved pet. By uniting with us, animals are learning to progress, and humanity has a great responsibility to them. If we show animals love and affection, they respond and grow into friendly and intelligent creatures. If, however, we teach them cruelty, then we not only invoke appalling karma for ourselves, but some of that karma rubs off onto the animal. If we turn them into guard dogs, make them perform in circuses against their wishes, or use them for laboratory experiments, can we blame them if the next time they reincarnate they appear as vicious and uncontrollable? Through their association with humanity they are evolving a separate soul, which in these instances is reflecting hate instead of love. Even more dreadful are the effects of this negative regression on the soul of the man or woman who instigated this enmity. I was at a country fair last year, where I spent an unhappy half-hour listening to a Master of Hounds talking to the crowd through a microphone. He was entertaining them with a lecture, the main ingredient being how much the fox enjoyed being chased by the hounds. What sheer fun it was for the fox to be torn apart by the dogs. What a wonderful death he had endured, all for the pleasure of a few people with more money than sense. This gentleman had, of course, been brainwashed since birth to believe such rubbish.

The animal kingdom should no longer have to sacrifice itself for the eating pleasures of mankind.

It has advanced too far on the path of evolution. When man ceases to eat his brother, the animals will follow his example. I would not dream of forcing vegetarianism on anybody who is not ready to follow that discipline. As White Eagle says, it should be done slowly and at our own pace. There came a time in my own life, however, when I could no longer see baby lambs cavorting in the field and then go home and eat them from my plate with mint sauce. To start with I gave up all red meat, only eating chicken or fish. Then I stopped consuming white meat, followed a year later by fish. Over the years my taste buds have altered and I now thoroughly enjoy my vegetarian fare. In our modern age we have many convenience foods to help us to adapt, and most public houses and restaurants include at least two vegetable items on their menus.

My body has never been healthier, due mainly to the fact that all the accumulated toxins from meat eating are no longer present in my digestive tract. When an animal is kept in factory farming units and then transferred to a slaughterhouse, the fear experienced by the poor beast remains in the carcass, and is then carried into the human body. So many antibiotics are fed into the farm animals that, again, when we eat the dead meat we store these drugs in our own cells, thereby weakening our own immune system. A good question to ask yourself next time you are about to eat your Sunday roast is whether or not you could perform the killing of that animal in the abattoir. If the answer is no, then should you really expect another person to commit that butchery for you? Free-range eggs are now so plentiful and cheap that there is no longer any excuse for devouring the products of a battery hen establishment. To be herded together in small pens, with no sunlight or fresh air, takes away the dignity of God's creatures. To refrain from dining on living flesh can spiritually enable you to take very large steps on the path of enlightenment.

Animals, as I have said earlier in this book, make perfect subjects for the energies of healing to pour through. It is a privilege to be able to serve the animal kingdom as a channel for this power. I have recently been helping a golden retriever called Sebastian, who had caught his foot in a rabbit hole, resulting in a very bad sprain to his back right leg. On the two occasions when I went to give him healing, he would place his injured paw in my hand before I had time to bend down and pick it up. He was completely receptive to the vibrations and knew exactly what I was trying to achieve.

There are many stories of heroism and devotion on the part of dogs and cats. A number of families have been saved from fires by the urgent warning of their pets. We have only to look at guide dogs to see the love from that animal transmuted into service. It is yet another way in which animals can rise very quickly on their own evolutionary spiral.

It has been said that bees and dolphins were given to us as a sacred gift from the inhabitants of Venus. The bees work for the vegetable kingdom by pollinating the earth, whilst providing honey for the pleasure of mankind. Dolphins, I firmly believe, are far in advance of humanity. Regardless of how we treat them, they love and show great delight in our company. They are showing this affection for us by acting as healing channels, and it has been discovered that mental disorders respond to the company of these magnificent mammals. After swimming with them, patients leave the water feeling calm and serene. Their depressions are lifted and they are able to return to their normal pursuits. Unfortunately, man is still wreaking havoc on the dolphin community, even teaching them to plant explosives on the sides of ships. If this continues, they will be withdrawn from this planet and man will lose their beauty and their companionship. Several marine experts are, however, working very hard to interpret their language, so that their knowledge can be understood and the purpose of their mission to this earth fulfilled.

I hope that I have thrown some light on the subject of unity between the three kingdoms of nature. If more appreciation was shown towards these realms, a glorious future would unfold before us. The Law of Balance would have control, and the Aquarian Age would see the spiral of achievement reaching up towards the summit of fulfilment.

JOURNEY INTO THE THREE KINGDOMS

As you sit relaxed and thoroughly at ease, become aware that your guardian angel is standing behind your chair, wrapping her wings of peace and love around your body. Feel yourself being lifted gently into the realms of light. For a short while you have no earthly worries; you have left them all on the ground beside your seat.

You have been taken to an area of boundless grassland. It stretches as far as the eye can see in all directions. Above you, the sky shimmers in the midday sun, which is an enormous ball of red and gold. The cloud formation rises up over the horizon giving the appearance of huge castle turrets.

In front of you is a magnificent oak tree, with its branches stretching way up into the air, so high that they are almost lost from view. This is a very old tree, the girth of its trunk being so wide that with your arms extended, it is impossible to encircle the sides. Its roots penetrate deep down into the soil, seeming almost to bring moisture from the centre of the earth. Slowly you are being lifted up into its highest branches. There is nothing to fear, the tree is welcoming you, forming a barrier of protection with its leaves so that there is no danger of you falling. You will notice that there is a natural seat for you to sit on, formed by the fork of a large bough. Take one of the leaves in your hands and study the formation of this intricate object. As you look at the veins and colours, it is as if the energy from the tree is passing through your hands. You have become united with the oak as it stands erect, guarding the inhabitants of its trunk and branches. You are aware of the insects and small animals who live within its shadow and give out to them your blessing and your love.

Your vision leaves the tree and you gaze across the grassy plains into the distance. You see wild antelope and zebras grazing and bathing in the midday sun. Suddenly something startles them and with their heads held high, the gazelles sniff the air before darting away across the savanna. As they leap and bound across the grass, their hooves hardly touching the earth, you are at one with them. Feel the wind rushing past your face as you rise up into the air before once more touching the ground lightly with your feet. You experience the sheer joy of being alive and becoming a part of all God's creation. There is no future, no past, just the eternal now.

You are once more back at the oak, standing against the trunk looking at the root structure. Its tentacles are pushing up out of the soil and are stretching away from the tree in a wide circle. There is a hollow in the earth, formed by the arch of one of these roots. Within the darkness something gleaming attracts your attention. You bend down, reaching your hand into the hole, bringing out a shining orb of light. It is a brilliant diamond, reflecting all the colours of the spectrum from its glistening facets. As you place this jewel against your heart you become a part of the love expressed by this revolving ball of light.

With this diamond held within your breast, it is only right that you should send this healing radiance out into the world. With your inner vision, bring into your mind a country engulfed in strife and warfare. Enfold the leaders and people of that land with rays of peace and love. Then visualize the minerals, plants and animals of that country who are equally in need of help and healing. Ask that balance may return to their realm and that the forces of light may reign supreme. You may want to irradiate several countries in this beam of harmonizing energy. Stay for a short while longer, before returning your thoughts to the oak tree. Put your hands against the trunk and thank your host for his care and safekeeping. As you send your love into the heart of the tree, feel the strength from this ancient initiate entering and filling your body with power and vigour.

It is now time to return to your everyday life, so gently and slowly come back into your chair. Breathe a little more deeply and imagine that your whole being is filled with the light of God's protection. Open your eyes and know that you are ready once more to continue with your life, holding within your heart the peace and fortitude placed there by the angels of the light.

A Celtic benediction

Deep Peace
of the running wave to you

Deep Peace
of the flowing air to you

Deep Peace
of the quiet earth to you

Deep Peace
of the shining stars to you

Deep Peace
of the Son of Peace to you

FOOTSTEP 11

Death, the Great Reaper

The one experience that no living creature on this planet can escape from is death. Rich, poor, famous, good or bad, all have to pass through the portals of that much-feared gateway. It is the main horror of most men, who would pay or do almost anything to free themselves from its clutches. Yet just stop for a moment and think; it should be the most welcomed event of our lives. Our studies for this lifetime have ceased, the term in school has finished and we are going back to our rightful homes for the holidays. We have passed some examinations but have failed to learn other lessons properly, so these must be taken again in some future incarnation when similar opportunities present themselves.

Death holds no fear for me at all. As mentioned in the first chapter of this book, I frequently travelled back through the tunnel of light during my childhood to play with friends on the other side. Death can be described as just taking off your coat, your outer garments and going into the next room. Life is indeed eternal with all of us moving upwards on the path of light, the spiral of evolving love and wisdom, until that great moment when we reach the mountain top and have no further need to reincarnate again. We then step into another dimension where new adventures await us as we again move onwards in God's great plan for our future attainments.

People say to me, 'But you have no proof of another life.' I then tell them the story of an experience that I had, which left me in no doubt as to the truth of life evermore. My grandmother, as I mentioned earlier in this book, was a spiritualist. I loved her dearly and missed her very much when she died peacefully at the age of ninety. She had always said that she would prove 'life after death' by coming back to either my mother, my aunt Sheila or myself. To my astonishment she came back to me. She had been 'gone' about two years when my husband and I were living in Hove in a flat over the top of our shop. I had been working very late the night before so had stayed in bed that morning while Peter went downstairs to start work. He brought me a cup of tea and when he left I sat up in bed to drink it. I was holding the full cup and saucer in my hand so I know I was not asleep. As I took a sip of tea I glanced at the open doorway at the foot of the bed. A slight mist had formed and I remember wondering where the fog had come from. I looked again, still drinking my tea, and was astonished to see a black handbag begin to take shape followed by a very familiar hat. Within seconds the whole form of my grandmother had built up. She was about the age that I remembered her as a child, very vibrant and very solid. This was the grandmother who had held and comforted me in her arms when I cried and had listened to my problems as a teenager. She left the doorway, walked round to my side of the bed, smiled and then bent over and kissed me on the forehead. I started to speak to her but she had vanished as quickly as she had come. I was still holding a warm cup of tea. I had felt no fear only complete joy; life was indeed without end. It was the beginning of a particularly harrowing period of my existence so as well as proving 'life after death', I am sure my grandmother had come back to console me. It was as if she was saying, 'Take heart, you are not alone, the trouble you are in is only fleeting – there is a light at the end of your dark passage.'

Several good Christian people have said to me, 'It's wicked to try to find out what happens after death. It goes against God's laws.' I totally disagree with these well-meaning souls. If I wish to take a holiday and travel to a particular country I borrow books, I read and find out as much as I can about the land that I am going to. So too with the planes of existence beyond the grave. I don't want to arrive on the other side ignorant and alarmed. I want it to be familiar and friendly. I am certain that this is also the wish of God, who for me is all love and has no desire that his children be frightened when they make the transition and start their greatest journey of a 'lifetime'. In this chapter I will, therefore, paint what I believe to be the true picture of the planes beyond death. Whilst asleep, with the help of a guide I have visited several different levels of consciousness in my astral body. This then is my explanation and description of the lands of light.

During the period of incarnation in our physical state, a silver cord attaches our earthly and etheric vehicles to our other bodies, i.e. astral, mental and spiritual. At death this cord breaks and we are able to leave our heavy dense and etheric forms to disintegrate and return to the soil of the earth and to the energy field surrounding it. This happens much faster if our physical frames are cremated rather than buried. We find that we are functioning quite happily in our astral bodies as we enter the tunnel of light to begin our journey onto the astral plane of consciousness.

It is a surprise to most people to find that they still have a body not unlike the one they inhabited whilst living on earth. They also see houses and buildings which look very much the same, although the vibrations are higher and everything appears much brighter. For a little while they may find themselves in healing temples and resting places, this stay being particularly necessary if death has occurred through terminal illness where pain has been prolonged. This peaceful period helps to strengthen their astral vehicles after the shock of passing over. They are treated with love and devotion by the advanced beings who work with the healing rays.

The astral plane is a realm of emotions and feelings and people on arrival find that their habits are very much the same as they were on Earth. On reflection, why should they be any different? Nobody becomes a saint overnight just because they have died. There is no spiritual law that says they must be perfect on arrival in the spirit world. There is no such thing as hell, only what we make for ourselves while on earth, which is reflected back to us when we enter the astral kingdoms. If we have been bright and happy whilst in our physical bodies, ever willing to help our fellow man, then we will gravitate to a light and cheerful area of the astral plane and meet with others of like mind. If, however, we have made life difficult for others, and have been very cruel, a torturer, an animal experimenter or a child abuser for example, then we will join others of similar tendencies in an area of greyness with very little light. This is known as the lower astral plane and proves that 'as we sow so shall we reap' even when we die. It is here that we will remain until we are able to feel sorrow for our deeds and begin to see the light of love. Much work is done in these areas of blackness and I have been taken in sleep to the lightest of these regions. I remember visiting a man who had been a very hard-headed businessman during his earthly life. He was still sitting in an office, working with a computer and answering the telephone. He was very happy to be in a place where he could still add up his bank balance and check his stocks and shares. He had known no other existence; he had no love for nature or beauty of any kind. He had always lived in a grey economic world and was quite happy to still do so. He would remain in this 'hell' of his own making until such time as he responded to the people trying to bring to him words of love and light. He was not a bad man, just someone with an obsession that had to be corrected. In a future life his business knowledge combined with compassion will probably be of great help to humanity.

Most people, however, will find that the astral plane is quite a pleasant place to inhabit. They will meet relatives and loved ones. Family pets will be waiting for them and they will still be able to listen to music and pursue pastimes that they enjoyed whilst on earth. The astral plane is also the realm of thought-forms, so they will be able, with practice, to build the sort of houses they want to live in or if they wish to visit another part of the area they will only have to send out a thought and they will be there.

The astral plane is not, however, just for lazing about and doing nothing. There is much work to be done and when they are ready, newcomers to this realm of light find enjoyment in helping others and learning at the same time. For the spiritually evolved there will be teaching, healing and counselling to be carried out, working very much with the brothers and angels of light. Although we have died, we can still give an enormous amount of support to the earth and its population.

Two areas of the astral plane that give much pleasure and happiness to those working in them are the lands for the children and the realms for the animals. I have visited both these kingdoms at night and will try to describe them to you. When I was taken to the land of children my guide was a little girl. After falling asleep I found myself in a valley with towering mountains on either side. Through the centre of this vale ran a small stream and it was here that this lovely child was waiting for me. I had a feeling that we had met many times in previous lives, but no information on this was given to me. She took my hand and led me over a small wooden bridge into the fields beyond. I was aware of great brightness and beautiful colours, some of which I couldn't describe as they are not of the Earth plane. I could see lots and lots of children of all different nationalities, some sitting in groups and some just playing. The air was warm and I could feel a gentle breeze against my face. I could see a number of buildings which were brightly coloured but seemed to be made of a transparent material open to the sky. I watched a group of little ones being taught by an elder brother. They were laughing and building colourful thought-forms in the air just as an earthly child would draw in a book or on a blackboard. My child-guide led me over to a dark-haired woman with a very beautiful and compassionate face. It was with this 'elder' that I spent most of the night. She talked to me and explained many things about this realm for children. In the buildings were the small babies and aborted foetuses who had died but who would all grow up in this land of light, reaching adulthood just as on Earth. Children who had been ill-treated and had never known kindness before they died were especially blessed. Here they were nurtured very gently and caringly, given great love and eventually taught to forgive and understand why certain dreadful acts had been performed on them. I was told that when the inhabitants of this plane reached maturity they quite often reincarnated again very quickly. Because of the special teaching and attention that they had had during their growing-up period on the astral plane, they are of great help to humanity during their lives on earth. They live to serve and are extremely spiritual. I wish all grieving parents could see how happy their children are when they reach the world of spirit. It would ease their pain to know that no child is ever lost or dead. No young lives are ever wasted; they are just living in another dimension. Love is the key which can link us with our dear ones when we sleep, and with practice this memory can be very clear and long-lasting on awakening.

The animal realm is just as beautiful as the children's heaven. There are vast acres of green grass with large leafy trees and many different varieties of wild flowers, some of which have never blossomed on the earth. I saw every animal known to us in the physical world, all living quite contentedly side by side. In this perfect environment the lamb quite happily lies down with the lion. As in the children's land there is a special place where tortured, ill-treated and frightened animals are looked after when they die. Their poor little broken forms are healed and for the first time they become aware of what love is all about. Many of us who respect the animal kingdom work in this area at night, cuddling and getting these shattered frames used to loving human contact. I have also seen men and women brought here, who were responsible for the cruelty wrought on these purest of God's creations, whilst working in the laboratories etc. on earth. It was their karma to work amongst these distressing scenes until they were able to feel compassion and love for their fellow creatures. God's laws can never be broken without the exact recompense being extracted either in this world or the next. There is no escape until we truly repent and ask forgiveness of ourselves, our God and our victims.

This brings me to an explanation of a hard lesson which has to be learned at some time during our stay on the astral planes. A compassionate and sympathetic elder accompanies us to a building where we sit and review our past life on earth. It is a time when we look at our mistakes and try to understand where we went wrong and where our lives could have been improved. The guide stays with us throughout this review, never criticizing, just giving kindly support and love. He knows our sorrow and our grief because he has sat in this seat many times himself. Our life flashes before us rather like looking at a picture show. Where we have caused pain and suffering through thought, word or deed we ourselves feel the pain within our own hearts. It is a harrowing and cleansing experience, leaving us wanting to make amends for these misdeeds. You will see now why it is important to ask forgiveness of others whilst alive and also the beauty of forgiving our tormentors just as Jesus did from the cross. It makes this particular part of our stay on the astral plane less painful. Much later, on a higher plane, we review the good and brighter areas of our earthly lives.

Having enjoyed the pleasures and lessons to be experienced on the astral plane, there comes a time when we realize that there is much more to be garnered in a higher dimension. We wish to visit the halls of learning, expand our knowledge and make use of our mental bodies. We begin to feel a pull towards the earth once more; to put right past wrongs and use our new-found understanding. First, however, we must learn all that we are capable of absorbing from the mental levels of consciousness. If we are at all spiritually advanced, we will have been cleansed of all negative emotions whilst on the astral plane, enabling us to experience the full power of love. This will help us to pass freely through the levels of the mental plane. Unevolved humanity is able to move around the lower mental realms with little difficulty, but on entering the higher kingdoms, they spend much of their time in a trance-like state, or in a light meditation, until they feel the need to reincarnate and join the human race once more.

Before entering this higher frequency there comes a period of deep sleep called 'the second death'. This is necessary to strengthen our vehicles and prepare ourselves for the raised vibrations that we will encounter on entering this advanced area of activity.

When we awaken we find ourselves in a land entirely different to anything that we have ever experienced before. We are in a region of pure thought, with very little solid form. We still have a body but it is practically transparent and very, very light. Everything is much brighter but the colours are muted, blending perfectly in harmony with one another. Here there is no rush or hurry, just a feeling of peace and tranquillity. There is no such thing as time; we can stay here as long as we choose to. Here we will meet masters and angels all working for the good of Mother Earth. The collective minds of these great beings unite to flood our planet with light, using the heart centres of advanced humanity to spread this love to every country and living creature incarnate on the globe.

We soon realize that this is the region where every idea or invention began. If, for instance, a new building is required in New York, the germ or flash of that idea starts on the mental plane, is drawn and given form on the higher astral plane and becomes a reality in the physical world. This is why we often find a solution to our problems whilst asleep; we have been able to visit the mental plane where the germ of an answer has been given to us. During our stay in these realms, we move from level to level developing our minds by visiting the teachers of wisdom and helping with the 'blueprints' for new ideas on Earth. This is where the progressive work for the evolution of our planet begins. New species of plants and vegetation are invented here, together with outline plans for the changing of the physical structure of the Earth in line with the coming ages of man. It is interesting to ponder on the fact that whilst dwelling on the mental plane, we are helping to form the conditions on Earth for when we next return.

As I mentioned previously, it is at some point whilst living in this world of light that we are called once again to look at our previous life on Earth. This time, however, it is a joyous occasion. We see all the good works that we have performed and share in all the happiness that we have given to other members of the human race. We see the results of seeds which we have sown, whilst helping others come to fruition, making conditions easier for those about to be born.

After we have taken in all the wisdom and knowledge of which we are capable, our souls begin to yearn, very strongly, to venture down into the Earth school for another period of study within dense matter. Until a soul becomes spiritually awakened, he will start his journey towards the Earth plane from this mental level. If, however, we wish to help with the advancement of our fellow man, we will have one more area of consciousness to visit; the lower spiritual plane. After yet another period of sleep, the third death, we find ourselves in a realm of pure light and only the outline of form. If we have gained a suitably strong spiritual body we will be able to enjoy our stay at this level of heightened vibrations, but for most people it is an experience spent in a dreamlike state. They will, however, absorb material into their 'light' bodies thus refining and heightening their vibrations for future use in another lifetime. If we have a particular gift which we are developing in order to help mankind, this is the plane where we receive instruction and help from the masters and angels. If, for instance, you have the ability to work as a healer, certain colours and shafts of light are woven into your spiritual body. You are probably working under an advanced being or master's influence, so instructions for your work are placed within your body of light. Soon, the pull towards Earth gets stronger and it is time to leave and commence our journey back through the levels of consciousness, arriving eventually on a very familiar, but at the same time, unrecognizable dense world.

Before we can start our new incarnation, we have to visit, again, each plane of existence, using the material and substance of that state of consciousness to build and sustain our various vehicles. First the mental, next the astral and finally the etheric level. These bodies are formed from patterns or seed atoms of all our previous lives. As we evolve, these are being made from finer and finer substances, making them stronger and fitter for each new lifetime.

The first plane we revisit is, therefore, the mental. Here we have much work to do. With the help of the angels of form, we alter and change the blueprint of our physical bodies to suit our new environment back on Mother Earth. We should never grumble about our earthly bodies feeling that perhaps our features are not as we would like them. We ourselves helped to design and structure them to suit this particular life. Any weaknesses or faults are usually built in from other incarnations. We meet with one of the Lords of

Karma to review past experiences to see where best we can pay off old debts, or where we can use our good karma to the maximum benefit of humanity. We can choose how much or how little we undergo; we have free will here, just as on Earth. We pick our parents and the time and place of our rebirth so that we can obtain the best advantage from our entrance onto the stage of life yet again. With all the facts before us, we are helped by the planetary angels to draw up an astrological chart of our forthcoming dip into matter. This is an exact outline of future events and whilst in incarnation any good astrologer, who knows the time and place of our birth, should be able to tell us what our lessons are and where best to use our talents. You will now see how important it is that babies should be allowed to enter our world in their own time and not at the demands of doctors or scientists.

After the completion of our work on the mental plane, we once more find ourselves revisiting the regions of the astral realm. From this area we are able to draw material to enable us to build a very strong astral vehicle. Through past experiences we have, hopefully, learned to control a lot of negative emotions like anger and jealousy. This fact, together with the depth of our ability to love and respond to positive feelings, is reflected in our astral bodies, thereby giving us a headstart in our forthcoming rebirth. Likewise, if we have failed to control our baser instincts this too is built-in and waiting for the opportunity to give us another lesson on how to deal with our darker natures. It is on this level that we will meet, talk and plan with our guides and angels who have elected to help us in the forthcoming years. It is like a small army gathering to do battle, using their hearts and swords of light to overcome the denseness and difficulties of life on our Earth plane. Never forget that this army is always with us, only waiting to be asked for their assistance.

With this phase of our work accomplished, we prepare ourselves to make the journey back through even lower vibrations until we reach the etheric region. As I have remarked earlier in this book, the etheric is the energy field of our physical bodies. Without this vitalizing force we would not be able to function and would become an inanimate object. You will realize, then, how important it is that we help the angels of form to build a strong etheric 'double'. The strength of the life-force flowing around our physical bodies determines how much help we are going to be to our fellow travellers on the path of life.

Our last task has been carried out and it is time once more, after many, many years of preparation, to enter our chosen mother's womb to await our birth on the densest of all the planes, Mother Earth. Our souls and our spirits are once more brought into action to await the experiences of life, which will build into them more and more light. Eventually will come a time when our bodies are so refined and full of light that we will no longer have a need to reincarnate. The wheel of rebirth will have ceased to turn and we will have become 'christed'. We are only then required to return to this world, at our own choice, if there is a special job for us to do, as did the Master Jesus 2,000 years ago in Israel.

Can you now see that life is a complete circle, from birth to death and from death to birth? The universe behaves in exactly the same way, with planets coming into birth and at the end of a vast cycle burning up and 'dying'. These great cycles of manifestation are ever evolving upwards and onwards; just a small piece of God's plan for man and the earth we use as our plane of physical existence.

THE TAPESTRY OF LIFE

If you have practised the previous meditations in this book, you will realize that they have all taken place within your heart centre and not your earthly mind. So for this journey I would like you to enter once more the cave that you visited in the first meditation after Chapter One. This is the cave within your heart wherein dwells the altar of wisdom and the candle of love. As you look out from the entrance to the cave, you will see three paths winding down the hill and disappearing into the distance. This is your journey for today. The walk will take you along one of these roads. The right-hand path represents the joys and sorrows of your life so far. The left-hand path indicates the way in which other people have treated you, be it for good or ill. The centre path portrays the positive or negative way in which you have influenced your fellow man. Pick one of these walkways and take your time in reaching your destination at the end of it. Ponder and reflect a little on the meaning of that particular road. Do not judge or criticize yourself or anybody else. This is just an exercise in the good and bad shades of existence. With most of humanity the bright patches outweigh the dull ones. As you tread your chosen path, you have the companionship of a guide who has been your friend for many incarnations. He is here to help you to look at the successes and the failures with equal love and understanding.

When you are ready you will reach the end of the road, which will lead you into a meadow full of wild flowers. Just ahead of you, you will see a small building which looks rather like a Japanese pagoda. It is painted in a delicate shade of pink that seems to shimmer in the sunlight. It has a warm welcoming look that draws you across the field and in through the open front door. Once inside you notice that there are glass windows all round that look out on to the meadow, letting in the sunshine. It is a happy, bright and cheerful room, which seems very familiar to you. In the centre of the floor stands a large tapestry with a seat in front of it. Your guide bids you sit and study the stitches and the colours of the wools that have been used. As you look at the picture in its wooden frame, you realize that it is a replica of your own life up to the present day. Some of the tapestry has been finished; parts of it are blank; some areas are brightly coloured, others are drab. You long to make the dark patches glow with life and wonder how you can do this.

Your guide takes your hand and draws you across the room to one of the windows overlooking the fields. Through it you see the path that you have travelled to get into the meadow. As you ponder on this view, you remember some of the people who have been hurt by your actions and you reach out from your heart centre to ask for their forgiveness. At the same time, with great compassion you send love and redemption to anyone who has caused you pain and suffering in the past. When your mission is complete you move back to the tapestry and with joy discover that some of the dull areas are now much brighter.

Your guide touches your arm indicating that it is time to leave, so you walk out through the open door and into the waiting field. For a short while just wander amongst the flowers and experience the peace and stillness of this scene. Sit on the ground and feel the warmth of the sun on your body. The sunlight is refreshing and filling you with energy and power. You have a sense of achievement, a realization that a weight has been lifted from your shoulders. In pardoning your enemies and seeking redemption for your own faults, you have been able to forgive yourself. In order to send light out into the world we have first to love ourselves.

You become aware that the scene in front of you has vanished and you are back in your own room, sitting in the chair and slowly opening your eyes. Your meditation has been a teaching in humility and acceptance. Although you have been looking back over your life, it is now time to move confidently into the future. Put your faith in the light from your heart centre, knowing that nothing can quench it and that love will always overcome any darkness.

FOOTSTEP 12

The Evolution of Planet Earth and Man

About fifteen years ago I experienced a very clear walkabout dream involving the possible removal of most of mankind from the face of our planet. My participation in this vision didn't last long, but it was dire, terrifying and very prophetic. I was taken to the scene of a battle, which I knew, intuitively, had been fought in a year just before the close of the twentieth century. Everywhere I looked I could see death and destruction. Nothing appeared to be alive, even the tanks and the instruments of modern warfare lay broken and strewn across the land. It was the utter silence that I noticed more than anything else, with spirals of smoke and fire rising from the ground like phantoms from some awful graveyard. I was then shown cities and towns lying in ruins, with a repeat of that uncanny quietness. No birds sang here, nothing moved except the dust being blown across an arid landscape. I turned in despair to my guide and asked why I was being shown such a dreadful picture. He told me that this holocaust awaited mankind if we were not prepared to change our materialistic habits. The Earth could no longer sustain our complete disregard for her welfare. He said that in the years ahead much effort must be put into opening men's heart centres, thereby reforming their attitudes, and averting the catastrophe that I had witnessed. In the same period as my dream, a number of books were written, forecasting the exact warning that I had received.

I have not spoken of this dream to frighten my readers, only as a prelude, before bringing to you a vision of a future filled with hope. Over the past decades an enormous amount of work has been achieved on the inner planes. Old souls have been reborn with the allotted task of building light centres all over the world. This has been accomplished, with prayer and meditation groups in every country flooding light into the dark corners of our globe. I have been told from spirit that humanity has been given a breathing space, a short time in which we must increase our endeavours to nurture and repair the damage to Mother Earth. I do feel that nuclear disaster has been turned away, but how much natural calamity befalls us depends on our exertions over the next few years. Our young people are trying very hard to build themselves a better destiny. We have organizations like Greenpeace and animal rights activists, all assisting in the promotion of this mammoth assignment. You may not agree with everything they do, but please stop and heed the essence of their message. Let us use vigour instead of apathy to become beacons of light for the well-being of forthcoming generations.

Next time you are in the open air, lie down on the grass and press your ear to the ground. Listen to the heartbeat of the Earth and harken to the rhythms of nature. Mother Earth is a very old friend, who has travelled alongside us for millions of years. When we started our journey, as a young spark from the heart of God, we spent aeons of time traversing the higher planes of existence. The Earth voyaged with us, structuring her own spiritual, mental, astral and etheric bodies. She followed exactly the same path as ourselves. When she reached physical manifestation, slowly hardening and progressing until she could support life-forms, we were not very far behind her. For vast periods of time, however, man lived primarily in his etheric body. His physical form solidified very, very slowly with scarcely any visible framework. This is why the 'missing link' has never been found. There were no skeletons for archaeologists to dig up.

The world, like ourselves, is a living entity. The Earth is the active manifestation of a greater being who uses our planet to gain further experience, exactly as we use our own physical bodies for the same purpose. Just as we have organs and cells within our vehicles allowing us to function, so does the Earth. The countries represent her major organs, the waters of the rivers and lakes are her veins and arteries, whilst mankind portrays the cells of her body. When the cells within her are in harmony, she is happy, but when the reverse occurs, she is exposed to disease. The forests and woods are her lungs and the flowers and shrubs her perfume. The birds, beasts and tides are expressions of her heartbeat, living in tune with the natural functions of her body. Birds migrate, animals hibernate and reproduce in accordance with the balance of the seasons and the magnetic forces that hold the planet within its orbit.

Let us stretch our minds a little further and ponder on our solar system. Our planet is, in turn, an organ within this even more illustrious entity, who employs our system as a physical materialization for his progression and evolution. Our solar system is, therefore, a part of an even vaster exalted being who is the Universe itself. Beyond this point our minds cannot fathom, except to assume that the spiral of experience reaches ever upwards and onwards, without a beginning or an end, into infinity. We are not only considering our own evolution, but we must remember that there are countless other angelic forms who rely on our universe for their advancement. There are seraphim and cherubim, Lords of various orders, guardian spirits, planetary archangels and nameless ones, far beyond the scope of our limited imaginations. If our planet allows us to destroy her vehicle, then we also halt and hinder the work of uncountable numbers of creations from way out into space, further than our imaginations can possibly stretch. If this looks like being the result of our actions, this planet will throw us off the face of the Earth with a shrug of her shoulders. As it is, our irresponsibility is causing an imbalance throughout the universe that must stop in the very immediate future.

So can you see what a great obligation man has to the world and to the rest of outer space? When we inflict wars on other countries and fight with each other, we are holding back more than just our own progression. Our dark and negative reactions are surrounding the Earth with formidable thought-forms, which, at some time in the future, will have to be cleared. Every one of us adds to this barrier when we succumb to our lower natures. If we could only remain positive and kindly towards God's creations, then we would be doing an immense service to ourselves and to our fellow travellers throughout the universe. Never forget that light always dissolves darkness and that one thought of love will overcome a hundred reflections of hatred. Armageddon, as I have written previously, will be the time when we have to turn and face these horrendous thought-forms and, with love, clear them from the proximity of the Earth.

Our planet loves us, as only a mother can, and she wants the best for her children. How do we repay her? We pollute her atmosphere, or breathing space; we chemically infest her rivers, or arteries, and we chop down her rain forests, which are her lungs. She therefore has no alternative but to begin to transmute, by changing her climatic conditions and the natural structure of her rock formations, causing earthquakes and land shifts. She is starting to do this slowly as a sacrifice to try to save mankind, by bringing to their notice the effects of their own stupidity. If unheeded, the results will be worldwide catastrophic devastation.

I adore humanity and our world, however, and am convinced that we both have a wonderful future together. When our Earth becomes a sacred planet of light so too will her children become beings of light. We will have earned the right to an inheritance of glory and grandeur. The road will be long and arduous, but the fruits of our labours will reap a harvest of dignity and vindication.

A relative of mine was very worried about the effects of nuclear waste that is being dumped into our seas and buried in our soil. She asked me if I would meditate on this problem, and enquire what the ultimate solution to this predicament might be. I did as she requested, and will share with you the answers that I received:

Nuclear power is an energy from God and was given to man by the spiritual sun. Humanity obtained this knowledge a little prematurely, but was allowed to develop its force as we all have to learn by our mistakes. Every step of the way was, however, closely watched. We are, at the present time, using it in a game of strength, with little idea of its true potential. It will be used towards the end of the Aquarian Age, as a spiritual tool for the advancement and enlightenment, not only of the Earth, but of the entire Universe. The mind of humankind will have matured to such an extent that a few men will be born who will be able to split the atom with their thoughts. This power will then be employed to heal and improve our lives, with uses of which we have no conception and cannot even dream about. It will heighten the vibrations of our bodies, allowing us to travel through space without the aid of machines. I was told not to fret and worry about the nuclear waste. Again, men would incarnate with minds powerful enough to destroy this radioactivity, or transmute it for honourable and moral undertakings. These occurrences would only happen, however, if man exerted himself at the present time, weaving a pathway of light for future centuries.

I was also given the information that atomic energy can be compared with the kundalini fire. This energy is aligned with the sacred centres of the Earth, waiting for the allotted day when it can be raised triumphantly, heralding in the victory of our Earth over the powers of darkness. Our world will only achieve this with the help of her human inhabitants. The ancient law 'As above, so below' is very true in this instance. Only when mankind has been christed, will our Earth gain her deserved award and reach illumination.

I am often asked the question, 'Does our planet have any negative karma?' I am afraid that the answer to this query is, 'Yes', and, as with humanity, it has to be cleared and worked upon. There are many brave and aged souls who have incarnated, with the single purpose of helping with this task. I have worked on several patients suffering from arthritis or cancer, to whom I could see with my inner vision that this theory applied. It is very difficult, however, for them to come to terms with the idea that their pain and suffering is aiding the cleansing of the Earth's karma. I gently make a few comments and leave my patient to reach his own realization of the importance of this revelation. This knowledge is usually deep within his subconscious, and only needs to be brought to the surface for recognition.

Before I conclude this chapter, I must bring into focus an evolved being who is guarding and helping mankind as never before. His name is Sanat Kamara, the last word meaning Prince or Ruler. He is one of the Lords of Flame, who initially came to Earth from Venus to help us to form a brain and thereby reach individualization. Because of his great love for all living creatures, he made the supreme sacrifice and elected to stay within this planet's influence, until such time as advanced humanity has reached illumination and can stand on its own two feet. It is said that he can hold the whole of the consciousness of mankind within his gaze. He pours down love, strength and courage onto all the four kingdoms of creation. The angelic and nature realms work under his command, as do the Masters and advanced initiates of all four life streams. It is through his guidance that great teachers have come to bring us instruction and watchers from other solar systems join him, from time to time, bringing universal light from far distant galaxies.

He can take upon himself a physical form, which gives him the appearance of a youth with flowing golden hair. His face is, however, so radiant that not everybody can gaze into his eyes without being temporarily blinded. Was this, maybe, the figure that Paul saw on the road to Damascus?

Sunat Kamara is also moving upwards on the evolutionary spiral. His participation in our advancement is preparing him for a large step forward on his own chosen path. Let us, therefore, in our meditations enfold the earth and this wondrous being in love from our hearts. Let us give praise and thanks to Sunat Kamara, for his divine and hallowed intercedence on our behalf. Without his help, we would not have reached that point in our progression when we could even begin to perceive his glory. Must all this intervention go to waste? Can we really repay his efforts by systematically destroying our planet? Of course not. If every person who reads this book spends just five minutes each day in meditation sending out love and light, our planet will reach salvation. We will all eventually stand before the

Lord of the World, knowing that we played our part in a huge transformation that was relevant to the whole Universe.

THE BLUEBELL WOOD

Once more, instead of a led meditation, I am including a poem for you to reflect upon. This beautiful verse was written by Joan Fugeman, after an inspirational vision whilst walking in the woods near her home. I am incorporating it in this book, as a tribute to her, for all the work she has carried out for the White Brotherhood.

Sit in your usual chair and when you are at peace, close your eyes and welcome the golden light that is surrounding you, lifting you upwards into the spiritual heavens. You see before you a wood that is filled with bluebells, drawing you into the sunlit glades. In the centre of the trees is a bank made of different types of mosses, forming a natural seat. For a short while rest and let the delicate colouring of the bluebells bring you comfort and peace. Ponder and contemplate on the words of this stimulating poem, whilst breathing in the perfume of the flowers.

> To walk alone in a quiet wood,
> Through the bluebell path where an angel stood,
> In company with a loving dog,
> Surely this way must lead to God.
>
> One sunlit evening long ago,
> In roseate sunset's golden glow,

An angel appeared in the bluebell wood,
In azure mist with wings of white
Enfolding her beauty in auric light.

In a time long past in a different place,
These paths were trod by another race,
Of ancient celts on their way to prayer,
Led by the druid priest to share
The first faint rays of the morning sun,
Through the silvery mist in this ancient wood,
Down the bluebell path where the angel stood.

The time has come when the earth must change,
And the will of man to God exchange.
Gone is the haze in the bluebell wood,
Gone is the path where the angel stood.
Replaced by the rubbish of chemical waste,
Trees felled to the ground in man's pitiless haste
To gain for himself material wealth,
Regardless of saving the planet's health.

Destroying the life in earth, water and air
Is dimming the life-force we all have to share,
And the beauty and love that man has erased
Is the heart of the land of this sacred place.
Oh Brother Man amend your way,
Before it is too late to pray.

But changes will come with God's infinite plan
For the cleansing of earth and the habits of man.
The greed and hate and selfish gain,
Washed clean by tidal wave and hurricane.
To make our home a better land,
In a golden age in time to come,

The earth will be cleansed of the dross and the scum,
And the amethyst light through the path in the wood,
Will still be the place where the angel stood.

FOOTSTEP 13

A Vision of the Future for Man

The most exciting part of this great adventure, mankind's journey back to God, is about to commence. We have left the infant school and are entering the junior level of our progression. The Piscean Age brought all our emotions to the surface, teaching us many lessons. Hopefully we have, to some degree, managed to control the passionate fires which in the past stampeded through our physical and spiritual bodies. Our astral vehicles should by this time be well-developed and more restrained. The Aquarian Age will focus new energies upon us, enabling us to begin to build strong mental bodies. This era will allow us to take a huge step forward, and our potential as 'Gods in the making' will advance a stage further.

The Earth, however, will not be so heavily populated as it is today. We will no longer feel the need to procreate in large numbers. Our sexual appetites will have diminished and our cravings for carnal pursuits will have faded. We will still enjoy liaisons, but in a more tender and gentle manner. We will learn to give as well as to receive. The true relationship between men and women, or even between the same sexes, will be understood. We will work to create from the mental level instead of from the fervent astral plane. Our love will still be intense, but at the same time dispassionate. This love will become unconditional and universal, not just reserved for a few close friends and family. Our bodies will become purer temples for our souls and our reproductive systems will only be used to bring into incarnation those members of humanity who can benefit from the Aquarian Age. A large proportion of mankind will be left behind, because they will be unable to adapt to the higher vibrations being poured down onto Mother Earth. You will again see, therefore, how important it is that we bring our minds into line with our hearts NOW and not at some future date. The stragglers of our race will, of course, progress on the upwards spiral, but it may be on another planet in some far-flung corner of space. Once again, I do not mean to frighten, only to quietly warn. It only needs a warm and sympathetic heart to make the grade and enter into the new age.

We are at the moment only using a very small portion of our brains. This wonderful computer has countless cells just waiting to be of service to us. Everything we have ever experienced is stored somewhere within this wonderful instrument. Nothing has been lost, but we have to mature sufficiently to fully appreciate the pictures that will be shown to us. Unfortunately, mental stimulation and growth will bring its own problems. The depressions and mental instabilities that are with us now will continue far into the new age. Our treatments should, however, have advanced by leaps and bounds. An Aquarian will have, intuitively, more insight into the cause of his own problems and if he is unable to put it right himself, there will be a wide variety of therapies open to him. Counsellors working with problems of the mind will be operating from a high mental level. They will have access to the akashic records and will see plainly what effects past karma is having on their patient. There will still be a need for trained surgical specialists but complementary therapists will take their rightful places alongside the physicians. Natural cures and remedies will become the normal rather than the alternative methods. We will gain considerably more knowledge about the use of plants and herbs, with fields and meadows being given over for their growth. Etheric healing, similar to the method described earlier in this book, will be used as a preventative and diagnostic tool. Colour healing will be widely used as a ray treatment, in combination with a psychological analysis of the qualities contained within the rays, appropriate to that particular patient. Large sunny treatment centres will be open to all of humanity, combining sports facilities with massage, sauna, and all known healing restoratives.

Slowly, over the years, man will lose his fear of death. His understanding of the other planes of existence will increase, bringing with it wisdom regarding his own immortality. Instead of doom and gloom, funerals will be replaced by celebrations of joy and happiness. We will have acquired the ability to slip gently out of our physical frame when our term in the schoolroom of Earth has finished. Once we lose our horror of death, then we will have no further need for spare-part surgery to keep us alive. Organ transplants will be ancient history and all animal experiments will cease. The animal realm will be given back its dignity and all exploitation in circuses and zoos halted. They will forget their fear of humanity, allowing us to walk amongst them, learning to communicate with this kingdom. Domestic pets will decide for themselves whether or not they want to share our homes. With freedom for the animals will come deliverance for mankind.

Our diet will also reflect our health. As we move further into the new age, the Aquarian will stop killing his brother for food and all people will be vegetarians. The slaughterhouses will be replaced by large organic farms. With a smaller population to feed there will be no starvation anywhere on the globe. We shall have more room to spread ourselves, so each household could have a large garden and be self-sufficient if they wished. I believe, however, that most of us will live in groups, sharing and providing for each other's needs on a global scale. Money will slowly lose its importance as it will be divided equally, thereby forfeiting its power over our thoughts. Fertilizers and pesticides will be banned, leaving the way clear for insects and worms to bring balance and health to the soil once more. The age of throwaway junk and chemicals will have passed, with recycling becoming a proven and basic law.

Teaching meditation and relaxation in every school will encourage healthy minds, bodies and spirits. In this way it will become a part of life and we will be able to explore not only other levels of consciousness, but other planets and past civilizations. We will begin to realize the enormity of the power that lies within our higher minds. The young will no longer wish to take drugs or sniff glue, for they will achieve the same euphoria through contemplation. Over the centuries, the atoms of our bodies will slowly become lighter and more etheric. The atmosphere of the Earth will also lighten, as we travel the same road towards illumination. When this starts to occur we will once again commune with the Masters and the angelic kingdom. There will be one government for the whole of the planet. Wars will die away and we will obtain the fulfilment of a prophecy, which is two thousand years of peace. Visitors will come from outer space and there will be a sharing of information and ideas. As well as world unity we will accomplish universal unity. Spiritual growth will put an end to personal desire and ambition, allowing the spread of love and compassion, with each man helping his neighbour to climb onto the next step of the path.

Even in Utopia, however, there is danger, as I was to discover when I fell asleep one night and experienced one of my walkabout dreams. I was met as usual by one of my guides and we journeyed to a distant planet that lay beyond our solar system. My first recollection was of walking through an archway, which had been carved and hand-painted, reflecting beautiful and strange hieroglyphics. We passed under these writings and I found myself in a land of light and wonder, with a population that was calm and serene. Everybody seemed happy and content, with no stress or anxiety to ruffle the smooth waters of their lives. Their faces were composed and untroubled, but in a strange way lacked character, with a rather wooden expression. They were very polite, but they never seemed to touch each other or give any sign of love or affection. For a time I thought I had entered paradise, but then I slowly realized that something was very, very wrong. Nobody really did a great deal or achieved anything. Their lives were static and terribly dull, just as if they had been standing still for aeons. An attractive dark-haired girl had joined us, also visiting this planet from another part of the galaxy. Before very long, she turned to me and said 'I can't stay here, I'm going home. This civilization is dying of boredom, their planet has stopped evolving and will soon perish.' She added, 'They have forgotten the words engraved on the archway.' When I asked her to translate them for me, this was the message that had been recorded:

> Curiosity is the saviour of Wisdom
> Complacency the slayer.

I had been given an accurate and authentic vision of a world and its inhabitants who had lost their ability to advance on the ever-expanding spiral of progression.

This is a lesson that man must never forget. It is our inheritance to surge onwards and upwards towards the next goal, always striving to overcome the obstacles which obstruct our pathway. In millions and trillions of years' time, the ancient wisdom tells us that we will have reached the stage when we will have become Gods. We ourselves will then have the ability to create universes from our own hearts and minds. 'What happens to us next?' I hear you ask. At this celestial and hallowed level, I am sure that we still advance to glories unknown and unimagined. Our infant minds are unable to conceive or envisage anything beyond this point but, as it stated over the archway, our curiosity will always urge us on to larger and more magnificent feats of achievement.

How, then, can man progress without the pollution caused by a large industrial community? With the birth of fewer people, wanting less commodities, the demand for huge factory units will diminish. We will again discover the satisfaction of 'hand-crafted' items. A system of bartering will return, whereby our simple needs will be met by various artisans working once more with the natural products of our Earth. Synthetic materials will no longer be considered practical or necessary. We are already discovering that certain plants can be grown and harvested in the fields to give us paper and fibre without the necessity to chop down our trees. Everything we require for our everyday use will be grown and nourished by an uncontaminated earth. The simple means of existence will be rediscovered.

Old mysteries from bygone cultures will once more come to light. Great and remarkable instructions to aid the future growth of humanity are buried at certain points around our planet. Some were concealed at the dawn of history by angels and helpers from other galaxies. Others were hidden by the priests of civilizations about to face extinction. In 1947 the Masters considered that it was time for mankind to unearth one of these buried 'treasures'. A Bedouin shepherd-boy was looking after his goats on the western shores of the Dead Sea in Israel. Whilst clambering over some rocks he discovered the opening to a cave and, being curious, tossed a stone into its depths. His missile happened to smash into an object on the floor of the cavern, which was a jar containing parchment scrolls. The lost library of the Essenes was once more to see the light of day, after two thousand years. Following the first excitement and much elation in the world's press, most of the contents of these manuscripts disappeared from public view. What should have been a celebrated revelation was thought to be too controversial for general publication. It was decided that the contents of these holy scriptures would upset the theological opinions and dogmas of our churches. Once more truth was set aside in the mistaken belief that it would threaten the origins of Christianity. Once more we showed ourselves unready for the unveiling of any more progressive knowledge.

This situation will change, however, once our true potential as spiritual beings rises to the surface. A volcanic explosion under the sea will uncover some of the secrets of Atlantis. Buried deep in the bowels of the Earth is an enormous crystal, which was used by the Atlanteans as a source of power. It gave light to their homes and worked the machines needed to grind their corn and weave their clothes. It has even been hinted that it provided the energy required to fly machines through the air. When we have advanced sufficiently, this gift from our ancestors will be found, and will give us a clean and safe means of fuel and transport. It will combine its power with the rays from the sun, bringing into operation the old ley lines and ancient stone circle sites. As Mother Earth yields up her secrets, the pyramids in Egypt and Mexico will once more glow and radiate. The esoteric meaning of their construction will be understood as the mathematical genius of their exact measurements in relation to the sun is appreciated. The chakras of Mother Earth will be revealed, allowing us access to their inherent significance. It is said that Great Britain is the heart centre of the world, so she will spread the energy of her love all across the globe. America will develop as the throat centre, allowing the next great spiritual thrust to come from her shores. In the far distant future what is now known as Russia will open up as the head centre, forming a magnificent triangle between these three countries.

The education of our children will incorporate all the mystical philosophies of the world, combining this with the history and geography of our lands. Science and mathematics will be used to prove the existence of other planes of consciousness, so the reality of these realms will be taught within our schools. Thought transference, healing arts, astrology and other occult sciences will all be part of their curriculum. The importance of laughter and recreation will be emphasized, making their classrooms ring to the sound of happy, gleeful children. Colour, words and sound will play a large role in the development of future generations. They will be able to bring through images and compositions from the spiritual levels, whose brilliance we can only hope to glimpse in dreams during our existing age.

Unfortunately, there will still be humans who prefer to work with darkness rather than light. They will see short cuts and experiment with Black Magic, seeking to use their powers to influence others. As they will be working from the mental planes, the forces they unleash will be extremely dangerous. Happily, the powers of love used by humanity will be far stronger, enabling us to surround and enfold them in this limitless might. At the end of two thousand years, we shall enter another great epoch, ruled by Capricorn. As with our present time, the transitional period will herald tumultuous changes. This, however, will not be on the physical plane. Battles of the mind will be fought on the mental level between darkness and light. This will be the period when the old negative thought-forms will have to be cleared from the perimeter of the Earth. Eventually the atmosphere will be cleansed and the army of God will have vanquished the dark forms. This struggle will be the forerunner for an ultimate victory thousands of years ahead of us, when light completely overpowers darkness. Satan will have finished his work and, together with his dark angels, will take his rightful place next to the throne of God.

It has been prophesied that the reappearance of the Christ will occur at some time during the Aquarian Age. I have pondered long and hard as to what form this new age manifestation will take. I believe that it will happen physically, as well as in the hearts of mankind. The Christ is a representative of God's pure light, which is love, compassion and devotion. Once this light has found its way into the hearts of men, then the road is open for the awakening of our brow and crown chakras. I believe that we shall meet the Christ on all levels of consciousness. He will bring with him a vast army of helpers, both angelic, human and galactic. Keys will be given to us, allowing entry into certain areas of the mental and spiritual realms, bringing knowledge and enlightenment.

The Christ is not only an illumination for Christians; he is the light for every religion and spiritual organization throughout the world. His coming will unite every belief and creed under one banner. East will meet West in the understanding that every road leads, eventually, back to God. This in turn will bring together countries, races and cultures under one banner. Discrimination between nations, colours and sexes will be unknown. Instead of separatism we will have unity, with humanity walking hand in hand towards an illustrious future.

As I have already mentioned in a previous chapter, the Master Kuthumi will act as a physical channel for the Christ light during the coming golden age. He will not appear until we have brought to this Earth a degree of balance, as it would be useless for him to manifest while we still torture and abuse the other three kingdoms of nature. Man must stop fighting his neighbour and cease from creating thoughts of hatred and intolerance before he will be able to appreciate the teachings of this ascended Master. His purpose on Earth during this age will be to lead us towards major initiations. This will not just happen to the chosen few; by the end of two thousand years, mass initiations will occur, enabling mankind to march confidently into the next great age of Capricorn.

This is the end of my story within the pages of this particular book. I hope the message that I have endeavoured to write will fill you with love and hope for the future. I ask you to join the ever-increasing band of pioneers, striving to avert the major catastrophes which are predicted for the end of this century. Open up your hearts and act as a channel for the peace which passeth all understanding. Together we will unite with the Lord of our Universe to bring in a future filled with joy and happiness. Let the heavens, and the whole of our galaxy, ring with the song of Earth. Let the love from our hearts shine forth as an inspiration for all travellers throughout the Universe.

AND MAY GOD BLESS YOU ALL

THE ANGELS OF EARTH, AIR, FIRE AND WATER

For your last meditation, I would ask that you raise your consciousness and return to the cave within your heart centre. Kneel before the altar and become absorbed within the light from the candle flame. The brilliance of its radiance has expanded out beyond the walls of this cavern, so that you can feel the vibration of love filling your whole body. Rest for a short while within the glory of your own heart. Let the peace and tranquillity fill every atom of your being.

When you are ready, step out from the entrance and look before you. Once more, a vision of the Earth has appeared, showing clearly the contours of countries, rivers and mountains. Your attention is drawn to the skies above, where many angels are beginning to take form. As they become clearer, you will see that they are composed of all the shining colours of the rainbow. Some are radiating the shades of nature, others the colours of peace or healing. All are enfolded in the golden aura of love and you will notice that they have gathered into groups, standing to the north, south, east, west and centre of our planet.

You are invited to join the angels who are standing to the north of the world:

> You see and unite with the angels of the sun
> And from their hearts flow the essence of life,
> As they unfurl their wings across the earth,
> They give to humanity the flames of power,
> And the energy from the sun enters the hearts of men.

You are next invited to join the angels who are standing to the west of the world:

> You see and unite with the angels of the air,
> And from their hearts flow the breath of life.
> As they unfurl their wings across the earth
> They give to humanity the winds of Wisdom,
> And wisdom enters the minds of men.

You are now invited to join with the angels who are standing to the south of the world:

> You see and unite with the angels of the water,
> And from their hearts flow the nectar of life.
> As they unfurl their wings across the earth,
> They give to humanity a river of love,
> And man opens his arms to the glistening waters.

You are again invited to join the angels who are standing to the east of the world:

You see and unite with the angels of the earth,
And from their hearts flow the sea of eternal life,
As they unfurl their wings across the earth,
They open the eyes of humanity to the vision of
eternity,
And man kneels before the glory of his Creator.

You are lastly invited to join the angels who are
standing in the centre of the world:

You see and unite with the angels of joy,
And from their hearts flow the music of harmony.
As they unfurl their wings across the earth,
They give to humanity the notes of peace,
And the melody of brotherhood enters the soul of
man.

The whole planet is now covered by a host of
heavenly angels and as you look the figures of the
Master Jesus and the Master Kuthumi appear within the circle of divine messengers. The Master of the
Piscean Age unites with the Master of the Aquarian
Age to bring deliverance to our unsettled globe. The
light of love streaming down onto the world is so
intense that you have to avert your eyes from the
brilliance. Your own heart centre has expanded and
opened to combine the blaze from your soul with the
radiance now enveloping the entire Earth. All darkness has vanished and only the exaltation of God's
blessing remains, as you see before you the miracle
of our world's transformation and redemption.

You gaze once more towards the Masters as they
raise their hands in praise and thanksgiving. You

are filled with a sense of divine contentment and composure. You realize that all your earthly troubles and problems are brief and transitory. They are just lessons that will pass and decline into insignificance.

This revelation dims and slowly fades away, leaving you once more within the cave. Rest for a short while, reflecting on what you have seen. It is a vision that you can use many times to succour and assist Mother Earth, helping to transmute darkness into light. In your own time, gently bring yourself back into your everyday surroundings. It has been a very powerful meditation so you must enfold yourself very strongly in a golden cross of light held within a circle of light.

The quotations used in this meditation have been adapted from The Essene Gospel of Peace, *Book Two, prepared and translated by Doctor Edmond Bordeaux Szekely, and are different from the original text.*

CONCLUSION

I hope my story has enabled you to realize that our physical lives are only a small piece of a much greater truth.

As I write these words I cannot adequately express the love and joy which fills my heart and flows out to all of you.

If I can be of help or service, please do not hesitate to contact me. I will do my best to answer any questions or queries that you might have.

You may wish to be put on my absent healing list, which I will readily do. The only thing that I ask is that you write to me from time to time with progress reports.

I have a list of workshops and lectures, which I will gladly send to you if you would like a speaker for your groups or functions.

Please send your letters, enclosing a stamped addressed envelope, to:

P.O. Box No. 1109, Portslade, Brighton BN42 4PP.

FURTHER READING

The Story of the White Eagle Lodge
The Quiet Mind
The Quiet Mind Companion
Spiritual Unfoldment 1, 2, 3 & 4
The Living Word of St John
The White Eagle Publishing Trust, New Lands, Brewells Lane, Liss, Hampshire GU33 7HY

Messenger of Light, Terry Lynn Taylor
Guardians of Hope, Terry Lynn Taylor
H. J. Kramer Inc., P.O. Box 1082, Tiburon, CA 94920, USA

Master Your Vibrations, Edmund Harold
The Spiritual Venturers' Educational Trust, P.O. Box 41049, St Lukes, Auckland, New Zealand

The Masters and the Path, C. W. Leadbeater
The Theosophical Publishing House

The Initiation of the World, Vera Stanley Alder
Rider & Company

Summons to a High Crusade, George Trevelyan
The Findhorn Press

New Age Healing, Brenda Johnston
11 Woodbury Avenue, Havant, Hampshire PO19 1RH

USEFUL ADDRESSES

Lorna Todd
P.O. Box 1109
Portslade
Brighton BN42 4PP

The White Eagle Lodge
New Lands
Brewells Lane
Rake
Liss   Tel: 01730 893300
Hampshire GU33 7HY   International calls: +441730 893300

The White Eagle Lodge (London)
9 St Mary Abbots Place
Kensington High Street   Tel: 0171 603 7914
London W8 6LS   International calls: +44171 603 7914

Crowborough and Brighton Daughter Lodge
c/o Mrs Avis Sheppard
Orchard Glebe
Ardingly   Meets in Tunbridge Wells,
West Sussex RH17 6UR   Brighton, Worthing and Eastbourne

The Sussex Healers' Association
The Deerfold Centre
233 Seaside
Eastbourne
East Sussex BN22 7NR

National Federation of Spiritual Healers
Old Manor Farm Studio
Church Street
Sunbury-on-Thames
Middlesex TW16 6RG   Tel: 019327 83164

International Network for Esoteric Healing
Dinah Lawson, International Co-ordinator
The Barn
4a Whichers Gate Road
Rowlands Castle
Hampshire PO9 6BB   Tel: 01705 412499

If readers wish to know more about the Essenes and other ageless
teachings, they may write for a free descriptive catalogue to:
International Biogenic Society
IBS International
Box 205
Matsqui
British Columbia
Canada VOX 1SO

THE EAGLE AND THE ROSE
Rosemary Altea

'A fascinating spiritual adventure ... Reminds us that our existence is more mysterious than any of us have dared to believe'
James Redfield, author of *The Celestine Prophecy*

From a young age, she heard voices whispering in the night, was visited by figures from the spirit world and at times felt as if the skin of her face was being peeled away by a threatening unseen force. For many years she kept such frightening experiences to herself until she met a group of people who would help her to realize her psychic gifts as a medium and healer.

In *The Eagle and the Rose* Rosemary Altea describes her journey into the spirit world through her Spirit Guide, an American Apache Indian. Grey Eagle taught 'his Rose' to use her astonishing power to heal, astral-travel and rescue souls lost on the after journey, and here we have case histories that illustrate Rosemary's remarkable talents.

Behind all these moving communications is the quiet, reassuring figure of Rosemary Altea, succoured by the wisdom and constancy of her mentor Grey Eagle. '*We are all souls and must trust each other with kindness,*' he says, emphasizing the true message of *The Eagle and the Rose*: we are not human beings having a spiritual experience, but spiritual beings having a human experience.

'One cannot deny the importance and truth the message of this book presents'
Bernie Siegal, author of *Love, Medicine and Miracles*

A Bantam Paperback
0 553 14112 7

A SELECTION OF NON-FICTION TITLES PUBLISHED BY BANTAM AND CORGI BOOKS

THE PRICES SHOWN BELOW WERE CORRECT AT THE TIME OF GOING TO PRESS. HOWEVER TRANSWORLD PUBLISHERS RESERVE THE RIGHT TO SHOW NEW RETAIL PRICES ON COVERS WHICH MAY DIFFER FROM THOSE PREVIOUSLY ADVERTISED IN THE TEXT OR ELSEWHERE.

14112 7	THE EAGLE AND THE ROSE	Rosemary Altea	£4.99
12138 X	THE HOLY BLOOD AND THE HOLY GRAIL		
		Baigent, Leigh & Lincoln	£6.99
13182 2	THE MESSIANIC LEGACY	Baigent, Leigh & Lincoln	£6.99
34539 7	HANDS OF LIGHT	Barbara Ann Brennan	£14.99
35456 6	LIGHT EMERGING	Barbara Ann Brennan	£16.99
40324 9	PERFECT HEALTH	Deepak Chopra	£9.99
17332 4	QUANTUM HEALING	Deepak Chopra	£9.99
18090 8	UNCONDITIONAL LIFE	Deepak Chopra	£7.99
40048 7	GOING WITHIN	Shirley MacLaine	£5.99
17201 8	OUT ON A LIMB	Shirley MacLaine	£5.99
40498 9	DANCE WHILE YOU CAN	Shirley MacLaine	£4.99
24452 3	LIFE AFTER LIFE	Raymond A. Moody	£4.99
40534 9	IN TOUCH WITH ETERNITY	Stephen O'Brien	£4.99
40718 X	ANGELS BY MY SIDE	Stephen O'Brien	£4.99
50310 3	A GIFT OF GOLDEN LIGHT	Stephen O'Brien	£4.99
11487 1	LIFE AFTER DEATH	Neville Randall	£3.99
40902 6	THE CELESTINE PROPHECY	James Redfield	£7.99
50370 7	THE CELESTINE PROPHECY: AN EXPERIENTIAL GUIDE		
		James Redfield & Carol Adrienne	£7.99
14214 X	BETTY SHINE'S MIND WORKBOOK	Betty Shine	£8.99
13671 9	MIND MAGIC	Betty Shine	£4.99
13378 7	MIND TO MIND	Betty Shine	£4.99
13998 X	MIND WAVES	Betty Shine	£4.99